CREED

CREED
WHAT CHRISTIANS BELIEVE AND WHY

Creed
978-1-7910-2788-9
978-1-5018-1372-6 *eBook*
978-1-5018-1373-3 *Large Print*

Creed: DVD
978-1-5018-1376-4

Creed: Leader Guide
978-1-5018-1374-0
978-1-5018-1375-7 *eBook*

Creed:
Youth Study Book
978-1-5018-1383-2
978-1-5018-1384-9 *eBook*

Creed:
Children's Leader Guide
978-1-5018-1370-2

Creed: Leader Kit
978-1-5018-2483-8

For more information, visit www.AdamHamilton.com.

Also by Adam Hamilton

24 Hours That Changed the World
Christianity and World Religions
Christianity's Family Tree
Confronting the Controversies
Enough
Final Words from the Cross
Forgiveness
Half Truths
Incarnation
John
Leading Beyond the Walls
Love to Stay
Making Sense of the Bible
Not a Silent Night
Prepare the Way for the Lord

Revival
Seeing Gray in a
  World of Black and White
Selling Swimsuits in the Arctic
Simon Peter
Speaking Well
The Call
The Journey
The Lord's Prayer
The Walk
The Way
Unleashing the Word
When Christians Get It Wrong
Why?

ADAM HAMILTON

CREED

WHAT CHRISTIANS BELIEVE AND WHY

EXPLORING THE APOSTLES' CREED

Abingdon Press / Nashville

CREED
WHAT CHRISTIANS BELIEVE AND WHY

**Library of Congress Cataloging-in-Publication Data can be found under the
original hardcover edition ISBN 978-1-5018-5421-7 (LCCN 2017471535).**

ISBN 978-1-7910-2788-9

MANUFACTURED IN THE UNITED STATES OF AMERICA

*I am indebted to theologians and professors
Charles Wood, John Deschner, and Schubert Ogden,
who served as my professors of systematic theology
in seminary at Perkins School of Theology,
Southern Methodist University.
They challenged me, stretched me,
and helped me and thousands of other students
to become pastoral theologians.
The shortcomings of this book are my own,
but to the degree that it faithfully and
intelligently conveys the truth of the Christian gospel,
it is in large part due to them.*

CONTENTS

CONTENTS

The Apostles' Creed

I believe in God, the Father Almighty,
    creator of heaven and earth.

I believe in Jesus Christ, his only Son, our Lord,
    who was conceived by the Holy Spirit,
    born of the Virgin Mary,
    suffered under Pontius Pilate,
    was crucified, died, and was buried;
    he descended to the dead.
    On the third day he rose again;
    he ascended into heaven,
    is seated at the right hand of the Father,
    and will come again to judge the living and the dead.

I believe in the Holy Spirit,
    the holy catholic* church,
    the communion of saints,
    the forgiveness of sins,
    the resurrection of the body,
    and the life everlasting. Amen.[1]

*universal

creed: noun \' krēd\ a statement of the basic beliefs of a religion; an idea or set of beliefs that guides the actions of a person or group.[2]

Introduction

I BELIEVE

Credo is the first word of the Apostles' Creed in Latin. It means "I believe." Before we explore what Christians believe, why they believe it, and why it matters, let's pause to think about belief itself. What do we mean when we say we believe? How does belief affect the believer? What are the sources of belief—the reasons for belief?

The word *believe* can have multiple layers of meaning and can be applied to everything from the silly to the profound. For example, I believe my favorite baseball team might make it to the World Series again this year. In this sense belief expresses my hopes, which may be at least partially rooted in my assessment of the skills of my home team.

Often we use *believe* to express our preferences or opinions or predictions about things that are not of ultimate importance. I believe a particular car brand is a better value than another. I would not die for my convictions about a car brand, and these might be easily changed if the right new product from another carmaker came along.

There are deeper and more important beliefs we all carry. You might believe that small government is important, or you might believe that government must do more to ensure the welfare of the people. You might believe that every citizen should have the right to carry guns, or you might believe that we need more restrictive gun laws. You might believe that one of the greatest threats to our future is global warming and that humans are having a significant impact upon the environment, or you might believe that global warming is a hoax or that it may be a real phenomenon but that humans have very little impact upon it.

Many deeply held beliefs have the power to motivate us to action, sacrifice, and service. I think of the convictions held by the Founding Fathers in the United States, who spelled out some of their fundamental beliefs with these words that nearly every American has memorized: "We hold these truths to be self-evident, that all men are created equal, that they are endowed by their Creator with certain unalienable Rights, that among these are Life, Liberty and the pursuit of Happiness."

Leaving aside the question of God for the moment, what are some of your most deeply held beliefs or convictions? How did you come to hold those convictions? For many of us, our parents played a key role in shaping our fundamental beliefs. It may have been a particular writer who shaped our convictions. Many of our beliefs have been shaped by personal experiences, particularly those experiences that most deeply touched our hearts—the most painful, but also the most loving, beautiful, or gratifying. These deeply held beliefs can shape us for good or for bad. Some fundamental convictions lead people to do great harm, and other beliefs lead people to live sacrificially in service to others. One set of convictions shapes the Ku Klux Klan, and another shapes the Sisters of Charity. What we believe matters.

From the earliest times Christians made attempts to summarize their essential beliefs. Beginning in the late second or early third centuries these summaries of the faith are found in the creeds of the Church. The most enduring of these, still studied and recited today, is the Apostles' Creed. I have used it as the basis of this book because it provides a concise and very early outline of Christian theology. While the Apostles' Creed likely took its current form during the 400s, an earlier version, usually called the Old Roman Symbol or Old Roman Creed, dates back to the second or early third century. I've included a copy of its text in the appendix, along with some other creeds of the church.

I wrote this little book thinking that many might wish to read it during Lent. Lent is the forty-day period of fasting, penitence, study, and spiritual growth that prepares Christians to commemorate Christ's death faithfully and meaningfully and to celebrate his resurrection. In times past, and still in some churches today, this was also the season in which converts were prepared for their baptism the evening before or early on the morning of Easter. Since the Apostles' Creed was likely written, and certainly popularized, for use at baptism, Lent was a central part of that preparation.

Our most important beliefs, whether expressed in the Apostles' Creed or in other ways, affect our understanding of what it means to be human and our convictions about values, morality, and relationships. Ultimately our most deeply held beliefs or convictions shape our goals, ambitions, hopes, and dreams. These kinds of convictions are seldom scientifically verifiable; nevertheless, we should carefully consider and question them and should be able to make a compelling case for them.

Since these convictions cannot be completely verified scientifically, there will always be some measure of doubt associated with them, some question as to whether they really are true. Regardless of what we believe about God, or humanity, or our world, we will lack certainty, and that lack of certainty should rightly lead us to humility in our convictions and in our interactions with those who disagree with us.

I appreciate Albert Einstein's words: "I believe in intuitions and inspirations. I sometimes feel that I am right. I do not know that I am."[1] There were some things about the universe that Einstein believed with a high degree of certainty, while many others represented reasonable convictions based upon what he could observe.

In the end, belief is a decision of the will. I choose to believe certain things. Thirty-five years ago I decided that I believed the tenets expressed in the Apostles' Creed. That decision has had a significant impact on my life every day since—on the person I married, the career I chose, the way I see right and wrong, how I parent my children, what I do with my time and money, and how I face adversity. Those beliefs have led me to say no to many things I may have said yes to, and to say yes to things I might otherwise have said no to.

For Christians, the beliefs expressed in the Apostles' Creed are foundational. In this book we'll consider those beliefs and begin a conversation about what Christians believe, why they believe it, and why it matters.

1.

GOD

I believe in God, the Father Almighty,
creator of heaven and earth.

Is there a God? How can we know? What evidence is there that God exists? Does it really matter one way or another? If there is a God, what is God like? These are the questions we'll consider in this chapter.

A GROWING REJECTION OF "GOD"

In the last thirty years, an increasing number of people reject the idea that there is a God. This growth in atheism has brought with it a number of vocal and at times hostile "evangelists" who seek to demonstrate that belief in God is absurd, anti-intellectual, even dangerous, and that the world needs to be rid of it.

Steven Weinberg, a theoretical physicist and atheist, once noted that "the world needs to wake up from the long nightmare of religion. Anything we scientists can do to weaken the hold of religion should be done, and may in fact be our greatest contribution to civilization."[1] A host of others have taken up the challenge; people such as Richard Dawkins, Sam Harris, Christopher Hitchens, and Daniel Dennett are among the best known and most vocal advocates of this position.

To be honest, I understand their convictions. When certain Christians insist on reading the creation accounts in Genesis as science, and adding up the genealogies in the Bible asserting that the universe was created less than ten thousand years ago, it is an affront to nearly every discipline of modern science. When Islamic extremists cry "God is great" as they detonate suicide bombs, it is easy to conclude that the problem is belief in God. When religious people study their scriptures and find commands that lead them to deny equality to women or to demonize gay and lesbian people, it is easy for the atheist to equate belief in God with injustice and ignorance. And these few examples don't begin to exhaust the reasons why people such as Weinberg have felt they were doing the world a favor by turning people away from God.

Is God, or belief in God, to be equated with anti-intellectualism, violence, and bigotry? Or would these very human impulses exist regardless of belief in God? After all, the officially atheist regimes under Vladimir Lenin, Joseph Stalin, Mao Zedong, and Pol Pot burned books, imprisoned and slaughtered millions, and fostered their own forms of bigotry. God or no God, human beings will find reasons to oppress and kill one another. They will resist progress in ideas, justify their own prejudices, and act upon those prejudices.

Just as Christians or theists might hold their convictions with a bit of humility, recognizing that the facts leading them to their convictions might have other explanations, I believe atheists would do well to maintain a similar humility to the question of God. Einstein articulated this well when he stated that on the question of God, he maintained "the attitude of humility corresponding to the weakness of our intellectual understanding of nature and of our own being."[2]

THE GOD CHRISTIANS BELIEVE IN

The Apostles' Creed begins, "I believe in God, the Father Almighty, creator of heaven and earth." Christians believe there is a God, a Supreme Being, an Ultimate Reality that created the universe.

Many would be willing to use the term "God" when referring to the creative and powerful forces that gave rise to, and hold together, the universe as we know it—forces such as the mysterious "dark energy" of astrophysics. When Einstein referred to God, it seems to me that he was willing to use the word in such a way—not a personal being, but an impersonal power or force, or perhaps a mystery of science yet unsolved. Yet Christians perceive God not simply as a force of nature, but as an entity, a Being, that is both intelligent and powerful.

Max Planck, the brilliant theoretical physicist and father of quantum theory, captured part of this idea in a 1944 speech in which he said, "All matter originates and exists only by virtue of a force which brings the particle of an atom to vibration and holds this most minute solar system of the atom together. We must assume behind this force the existence of a conscious and intelligent mind. This mind is the matrix of all matter."[3] Planck, a Nobel Laureate, did not see his work in the field of quantum mechanics as incompatible with his Christian faith. Sustaining and holding the universe together was an almighty force that was both "conscious" and "intelligent."

George Lemaître, a Catholic priest and cosmological physicist, was perhaps best known as the father of the Big Bang theory. He championed the idea that the universe had a beginning, a day on which it was born. His theory of cosmic expansion pointed backward to "a day when there was no yesterday." Lemaître did not see this idea as proof of God's existence, but he did seem to recognize that his theory, now widely accepted, made it intellectually possible to reconcile faith and science.

There are many scientists who believe that science and faith are incompatible, but many others throughout history have believed, and continue to believe, that the two are not mutually exclusive. During the "scientific revolution" of the sixteenth and seventeenth centuries, for example, some of the leading luminaries were Christian believers—people such as Isaac Newton, Blaise Pascal, and Galileo, who, despite the church's blunder in criticizing his conclusions, continued to maintain his faith in God.

My point is that, despite frequent statements by some scientists that science and Christian faith are incompatible, there are numerous other scientists who have played significant roles in the advancement of knowledge *and* who believed in God, the Father Almighty, creator of heaven and earth.

Christians believe that God is the creative force, the power, the source from which everything that exists derives its existence and upon which all that exists is contingent.

We see this idea in the name by which God reveals himself to Moses in Exodus 3:13-14. There God speaks to Moses in the midst of the wilderness of Sinai. A voice speaks from a burning bush. God calls Moses to lead the children of Israel, slaves in Egypt, to freedom and the Promised Land. Moses, who lives in a polytheistic world, says to the voice, "[The Israelites] are going to ask me, 'What's this God's name?' What am I supposed to say to them?" In other words, Moses is asking, "Of all the many deities people worship, which one are you?" In response,

> God said to Moses, "I Am Who I Am. So say
> to the Israelites, 'I Am has sent me to you.'"

This phrase, *I Am Who I Am*, is in Hebrew a wordplay on the proper name Yahweh (or Jehovah), usually rendered in English Bibles as LORD. What kind of name is I Am? I believe that God is revealing himself to Moses, and through Moses to Israel, as being itself, the source of all that is, from which everything that is has come to be and continues to be.

Here's where theology and physics might meet. Physicists speak of fundamental forces (strong, weak, gravity, and electromagnetic) that are responsible for governing, shaping, and sustaining the universe. They speak of particles that permeate the universe, and of things such as dark energy and dark matter, most of which cannot be seen and are not yet fully understood but which play a critical role in forming and sustaining the universe we inhabit.

When I hear physicists talking about these things they cannot see, which cannot be fully explained but which permeate the universe, which make possible all that exists, I can't help thinking of Paul speaking in Athens to the leading philosophers of that city. Paul described God as the one who made the world and everything in it, and then went on to quote the sixth-century-B.C. Greek philosopher-poet Epimenides, who wrote, "In him we live and move and have our being" (Acts 17:28 NRSV).

Many physicists accept and occasionally use the term "God" as shorthand for describing the mysterious, invisible forces that govern the universe, but Christianity doesn't stop there. Christians also see God as a being, an entity with all the attributes of personhood: intelligence, emotion, reason, logic, and will. God knows, feels, loves, thinks, wills, acts, and creates. The Creed, drawing from Jesus' primary way of addressing God, speaks of God as Father, a very personal, intimate, and relational term. God is the force and power behind everything, *and* God is a being who defines the very meaning of personhood. Whatever makes us persons, Christians believe, is derivative of or a reflection of God's personhood. Scripture writers describe this belief by saying that human beings were created in the *Imago Dei*—the image of God.

So when we look at the universe as it is, we see a reflection not just of the random functioning of various forces, but a reflection of the creativity, joy, beauty, and majesty of the One who has created.

EVIDENCE FOR GOD?

Christians (and other theists) believe in God. But is there any evidence that God exists? Is there good reason to believe?

Throughout most of human history, the argument for God's existence, the case for God, started with the fact that the universe exists and that we exist. It seemed unthinkable to most human beings that the beauty and majesty of creation should either (a) have always existed without a beginning or (b) have spontaneously generated out of nothing with no One to create it. Further, the order evident in creation—the natural laws, the complexity of what we can observe, including human beings capable of reason—seem further evidence of a Being, a Mind behind the creation of the cosmos.

Those who reject the idea of God make the case, as cosmologist Lawrence Krauss does in his best-selling *A Universe from Nothing*, that the universe could exist without an external force. I appreciate Krauss's book. I love astronomy and am fascinated by astrophysics and cosmology (though I admit there are ideas in the field that make my brain hurt and which I don't fully comprehend!).

I have a telescope, and I love to take it out in the backyard on dark nights, turning my gaze to planets, stars, star clusters, nebulae, and galaxies. As I peer through the eyepiece, I see the light of stars that took thousands and in some cases millions of years to reach my eye. Inevitably I find myself thinking how magnificently large our universe is, and how small my part in it is. Often my mind returns to the words of Psalm 8:3-4.

> *When I look up at your skies,*
> *at what your fingers made—*
> *the moon and the stars*
> *that you set firmly in place—*
> *what are human beings*
> *that you think about them;*
> *what are human beings*
> *that you pay attention to them?*

Reading Krauss and others helps me understand the scientific data and the current theories of cosmology and astrophysics. I am fascinated by them. But none of these leads me to Krauss's conclusion that there is no God. Perhaps it's because, as Krauss notes in his book, "Data rarely impress people who have decided in advance that something is wrong with the picture."[4] But if his contention applies to Christians and other theists, I think it also applies to atheists. The question of God is unlikely to be resolved by science. Theists and atheists can look at the same data and reach different conclusions. I see the fingerprints of God when I read the work of scientists. To me, the mysterious, invisible forces that gave rise to our universe and hold it together seem to be the handiwork of God; the scientist simply uses a different name.

I also see the guiding hand of God in the evolution of our universe. Narrow the focus to life on our planet and, once again, I see the handiwork of God. I grasp and accept that Darwin's theory of evolution is a brilliant and helpful way of understanding the differentiation of life on our planet. But knowing the mechanism (evolution) does not therefore disprove that there was One who designed the mechanism and worked through it. Reading Darwin doesn't diminish my conviction that there is something more at play in the development of life on our planet than just evolution.

Oxford mathematician John Lennox notes that the odds for the self-organization of life on earth are in the neighborhood of 1 to 10 to the 40,000 power—very slim odds indeed. Astronomer Fred Hoyle suggested an often-cited analogy for the improbability of life on earth organizing on its own, saying the chances were about the same as those of a gale-force wind blowing through a junkyard and, after it passed, revealing that a Boeing 747 had spontaneously assembled itself.[5]

A simpler analogy might be to inquire what it would take for cocoa, eggs, flour, sugar, and oil to assemble themselves spontaneously into a three-layer chocolate cake. No matter how many billion years we might wait, there will be no three-layer chocolate cake without its being mixed, baked, and iced by someone who knows what a chocolate cake should look and taste like.

Here's my point: when the atheist considers the universe, our planet, and life on the planet, there will always be a natural explanation that does not require God—some x-factor that helps to explain the inexplicable. (Today, so-called multiverses are a popular x-factor thought by many to hold a key.) To the theist, the truth inevitably lies one layer beyond these explanations, because every solution proposed by the scientific community points to the need for another x-factor.

For Christians this x-factor, this unseen force behind the existence and development of the universe, is God.

This fundamental disagreement in how we explain the origins of all that is cannot ultimately be resolved, and that is why debates between atheists and theists are usually unsatisfying and do little to persuade the unpersuaded on either side. Ultimately these debates come down to who got the better sound bite, who came up with the quickest and best response, or who did a better job of thinking on their feet. But in the end the atheist has chosen a belief, a creed, as has the Christian. Both look at the same data and reach different conclusions.

As a Christian, I see God's glory and creativity throughout creation. The atheist, looking at the same things, sees the glory and creativity of nature. At some point we choose either to believe or to reject the idea that there is One whose power and mind have brought forth the cosmos. Paul was one who believed that the universe itself points to the existence of God: "Ever since the creation of the world, God's invisible qualities—God's eternal power and divine nature—have been clearly seen, because they are understood through the things God has made" (Romans 1:20). Likewise the psalmist writes:

> *The heavens declare the glory of God;*
> *the skies proclaim the work of his hands.*
> *Day after day they pour forth speech;*
> *night after night they reveal knowledge.*
> *They have no speech, they use no words;*
> *no sound is heard from them.*

Yet their voice goes out into all the earth,
their words to the ends of the world.
(Psalm 19:1-4 NIV)

When I look at the magnificent deep-space images from the Hubble Space Telescope, I am grateful to know a bit of the science behind what I'm looking at, yet I still cry out with the psalmist, "LORD, our Lord, how majestic is your name in all the earth!" (Psalm 8:1 NIV). I say the same when, at the opposite end of the scientific scale, I look at the amazing patterns created when subatomic particles interact at the Large Hadron Collider, the largest and most powerful particle collider ever built. I feel it when I look at the patterns of a snowflake, just as I do when I consider the amazing software that instructs a fertilized egg to develop into a human being.

I believe in God in part because I am; because I think and reason and love and perceive. I believe that my very existence, and yours, points to something greater than we are. But beyond the simple and wonderful fact of existence, there are other things that lead me to believe there is One who exists and by whom we exist, and who at one and the same time is greater than the universe and nearer than the air I breathe.

I believe because of the thousands of moments in prayer, Scripture reading, and reflection when I've felt something— Someone—offering comfort, assurance, guidance, and grace. Something within me needs to trust, to give thanks, to praise, to worship One who is greater than myself. I believe this is so because there is One for whom I was made, whose intent in creating humanity was that we might be in relationship with him.*

I feel connected with God when I take a long walk and pause to give thanks. I feel deep peace in the midst of physical and emotional storms when I have turned to God in prayer. I feel most fully alive when I am doing the things Jesus described as God's will. When singing and praying and listening in worship, I inevitably hear God speaking to me, or feel my heart connecting with him. I'm aware that the atheist has explanations for all of these: chemicals washing across my brain, or a "God gene" that causes me to have spiritual and mystical experiences, or simply wishful thinking. To me, the simplest explanation is that these experiences point to something, or Someone, that is real.

In my life I often experience coincidences that seem to involve more than chance—intuitions to do something, to call someone, to go somewhere. Hundreds of times I've done the thing I've felt nudged to do, and I find myself in a place where I was needed or where I needed to be. These "coincidences" seem more often, to me, to be "God-incidences." Over the years I've come to trust that there is One who nudges us, guides us, and leads us if we pay attention. I'll speak more of these nudges when we discuss the Holy Spirit later in this book.

At one time, as a teenager, I did not believe there was a God. I had arguments commensurate with a boy's intellect and experience that led me to this conclusion. As I grew up,

---

* God is not strictly male but transcends and encompasses both male and female; however, here and elsewhere in this book I'll use the pronouns for God used in the Creed.

however, I came to believe in God, at first I suppose because of the witness of others who believed in God. They claimed to have had experiences similar to those I've just described in my own life. This led me to read the Bible. The Bible is a library of documents containing the various authors' reflections and experiences of God. It was in reading about the life of Jesus in the Gospels that I found myself drawn to this man. Jesus, whom many nonbelievers profess admiration for, believed in God. In a sense I came to believe there was a God because I trusted Jesus and he believed in God!

I believe in God because, though Darwin got many things right in his classic work *On the Origin of Species*, humans demonstrate an interesting capacity to violate the laws of natural selection in how we live as a species. When we care for the weak, when we are faithful to a spouse, when we show compassion to the struggling, when we choose to love our enemies, we are acting counter to the laws of natural selection but consistent with an inner law written on our hearts that we intuitively know is the right and good path. I believe that this inner law, which reflects humanity at its best, points to the One in whose image we were created.

None of what I've just shared proves God's existence. If you are a committed atheist, you are likely already formulating arguments against what I've said. We each weigh the same data and our experiences and reach our own conclusions upon which we build our convictions. But when it comes to the foundation I choose to build my life on, I am led by my experiences, by the intuitions and intimations in my soul, by the fact of existence, and by the witness of Jesus Christ to repeat these familiar words: "I believe in God, the Father Almighty, creator of heaven and earth." And as I hear scientists describe the unseen forces that permeate the universe, that gave rise to it and sustain it, I often think that perhaps they too have found, without knowing it, the presence, essence, and power of God.

WHY FAITH IN GOD MATTERS

My aim in this book is not only to describe what Christians believe and their reasons for believing it, but to consider why these beliefs matter. So, if one accepts that belief in God is reasonable and consistent with our observations about the universe and our experiences as human beings, what difference does this make? For many people, very little. Sometimes those who believe but whose lives are not affected by this belief are called "practical atheists"—people who live their daily lives as though there is no God while giving mental assent to the idea of God.

But belief in the sense that the Creed intends is not merely mental assent to a particular idea. It is, as defined earlier, "an idea or set of beliefs that guides the actions of a person or group." For those who shaped the Apostles' Creed, belief in God is meant to fundamentally change our perspective on the world, on our place in it, and on our own lives. If there is a God, then we are creatures who are not nearly as important in the scheme of things as we might think.

I love how the psalmist captures this perspective:

Lord, you have been our help,
generation after generation.

Before the mountains were born,
before you birthed the earth and the
inhabited world—
from forever in the past
to forever in the future, you are God.

You return people to dust,
saying, "Go back, humans,"
because in your perspective a thousand years
are like yesterday past,
like a short period during the night watch.
You sweep humans away like a dream,
like grass that is renewed in the morning.
(Psalm 90:1-5)

This view promotes a certain humility about our lives and their relative importance. Interestingly, the same view is offered by a right understanding of science. According to both views, each of us is quite small in the scheme of things. But a belief in God as both creator and Father adds something to our smallness. We are small and seemingly insignificant in the scheme of things, and yet we matter to God. Scripture not only speaks of God as Father, but of us human beings as God's children.

Christianity teaches that we are known and even loved by God. It teaches that we bear in our minds and souls the image of God. To complement the psalmist's teaching that we return to dust, the Bible also teaches that we have value and worth as human beings. We are not to kill one another. We are to treat one another as we wish to be treated. We are to love one another. We are to bear one another's burdens and to work for justice while demonstrating mercy. Why? Because our fellow human beings matter to God, as we do. We are not expendable cogs in an evolutionary machine. We are children of God.

If there is a God, and you and I are his creatures, then the appropriate response, according to the Scriptures, is praise, gratitude, and worship. We are to love God with all our heart, mind, soul, and strength. When I wake up in the morning, thanksgiving for a new day should be on my lips. When I lie down to sleep, I should offer thanksgiving for the day that has passed. Each day is a gift. Each good experience a blessing. In an ultimate sense, everything good in life is an act of God's grace. Faith in God leads us to humility, but it also leads us to gratitude.

Belief in God also has huge implications for our care of creation. If God created all things, and the earth belongs to God, then we are stewards of it. Many think of Christian discipleship and spirituality as reading the Bible and praying, and these are important; but if this earth really belongs to God, then caring for it—tending God's garden—is an act of discipleship and a responsibility of every human being. When you leave a room, turning off the lights is an act of faithfulness and Christian discipleship. So, too, is turning up the thermostat, recycling, and thinking about fuel economy when you buy your next car. Conversely, damaging the earth or wasting its resources is an affront to the Creator. Belief in God should lead us to caring for God's creation.

But believing in God goes beyond that. If God exists, then my aim is to understand God's will for how I should live as a human being. Christians find God's will in studying the Scriptures, particularly the life and teachings of Jesus. Jesus calls us to rise above our animal instincts. He calls us to love our neighbor, even our enemy. He calls us to forgive rather than seek vengeance, to overcome evil with good, to do justice and practice lovingkindness. Christians see themselves in daily pursuit of God's mission in the world. To be authentically human is to know God's will and do it. And in this we will find a deep satisfaction in life.

There's more: if God exists, and God is as the Scriptures describe him, then we are never alone. As the psalmist so beautifully notes, even when we walk through the valley of the shadow of death, we need fear no evil, for God is with us. Over one hundred times in Scripture the biblical authors tell us not to be afraid, for God is with us. If God exists, there is always hope. This is an idea we'll return to in subsequent chapters.

These observations just scratch the surface of how belief in God matters. Each successive chapter will point to other ways in which Christian faith is meant to fundamentally, profoundly, and positively affect those who believe and the world in which we live.

I've read enough writings of atheists to know how they might brush aside all these arguments in making the case for their own creed. They would not likely come to faith as a result of my arguments, any more than I would lay aside my faith because of theirs. In the end we each have to weigh the data we have, including the world as it is, our experiences as they are, and the witness of those around us, and then decide whether or not we choose to believe. But just as Krauss, Dawkins, and other leading atheists would encourage believers to keep an open mind, I would encourage atheists to hold their skepticism with humility and make room for the possibility that there really is a God.

Recently I was in London walking through St. Paul's Cathedral, a magnificent structure designed by Christopher Wren following the Great Fire of 1666. Construction began in 1675 and took forty-five years to complete. The dome rises to 365 feet, making it one of the highest in the world.

In the bowels of the church are crypts where a number of famous people from centuries past are buried. Many of the crypts have detailed statuary with amazing ornamentation. But on one wall is a rather plain marker, easily missed, upon which are written these words:

> Here in its foundations lies the architect of this church and city, Christopher Wren, who lived beyond ninety years, not for his own profit but for the public good. Reader, if you seek his monument—look around you.

The evidence that Christopher Wren lived can be seen in the cathedral, as well as in building after building in London that he designed and built. Many people visit the city without knowing about Wren. Some visit the church and never see his grave. But the evidence of his existence and importance is clearly displayed throughout London. The same, I believe, can be said about God as we look around us at the magnificent world God has created.

2.

JESUS CHRIST

I believe in Jesus Christ, his only Son, our Lord,
who was conceived by the Holy Spirit,
born of the Virgin Mary,
suffered under Pontius Pilate,
was crucified, died, and was buried;
he descended to the dead.
On the third day he rose again;
he ascended into heaven,
is seated at the right hand of the Father,
and will come again to judge the living and the dead.

Hindus, Muslims, Jews, and the vast majority of the world's people believe there is a God. What sets Christianity apart from these other faiths is its specific beliefs about Jesus. Some of the world's religions affirm that Jesus was a prophet, an important teacher, or a religious reformer. Even among atheists there is general agreement that Jesus was, as popular atheist Richard Dawkins affirms, a "great moral teacher."[1] Christianity affirms that Jesus was indeed a prophet, religious reformer, and great moral teacher, but the Christian faith says far more than this.

Scholars describe the part of Christian theology focused on the beliefs about Jesus as Christology. In this chapter we'll consider some of the Christological beliefs of mainstream Christianity: what Christians believe about Jesus, why they believe it, and why it matters.

SOURCES OF INFORMATION ABOUT JESUS

Let's begin with a brief word about how we know what we know about Jesus. Jesus didn't leave any written documents; most of the people he ministered with could not read or write. There are very few Roman documents in existence from the first half of the first century, and we would not expect any to record the crucifixion of a Jewish peasant in what was considered the backwaters of the Roman Empire. Flavius Josephus wrote a comprehensive history of the Jews for the Romans near the end of the first century, and his works contain several references to Jesus.* After the turn of the first century, the Roman senator and historian Tacitus mentioned Nero's

---

* The following is the most detailed mention of Jesus in *The Antiquities*, 18:3:3, but scholars debate how much of this was original to Josephus and how much was expanded by later editors: "Now there was about this time Jesus, a wise man, if it be lawful to call him a man; for he was a doer of wonderful works, a teacher of such men as receive the truth with pleasure. He drew over to him both many of the Jews and many of the Gentiles. He was [the] Christ. And when Pilate, at the suggestion of the principal men amongst us, had condemned him to the cross, those that loved him at the first did not forsake him; for he appeared to them alive again the third day; as the divine prophets had foretold these and ten thousand other wonderful things concerning him. And the tribe of Christians, so named from him, are not extinct at this day."

persecution of the Christians in Rome and noted that Christ was crucified under the reign of Pontius Pilate in Jerusalem.

The earliest and most extensive information we have concerning Jesus comes from the twenty-seven documents of the New Testament, nearly all of which were written between A.D. 50 and 95, including the four Gospels: Matthew, Mark, Luke, and John. These Gospels, written by Jesus' followers and drawing upon material from a variety of sources, offer a great deal of information about Jesus.

Luke begins his Gospel with the following prologue, in which he describes his intent in writing and something of the process by which he wrote. These words help scholars to know that, prior to the publication of Luke's Gospel in the 70s or 80s, there were others who had written about Jesus, and Luke drew upon these earlier sources:

> *Many people have already applied themselves*
> *to the task of compiling an account of the*
> *events that have been fulfilled among us.*
> *They used what the original eyewitnesses and*
> *servants of the word handed down to us. Now,*
> *after having investigated everything carefully*
> *from the beginning, I have also decided to*
> *write a carefully ordered account.*
> *(Luke 1:1-3)*

The Gospels are not strictly biographies of Jesus, though they are biographical in nature, describing what Jesus said and did. They were written by people who had come to believe that Jesus was the Christ, God's Son and their Lord—that is, by Christians for Christians, or for those open to becoming Christians. The scholarly consensus is that the Gospels were written between A.D. 70 and 90 but can be demonstrated to draw upon earlier sources and, as Luke notes, eyewitness accounts of Jesus' life. They paint a remarkably consistent account of Jesus' life, death, and resurrection.

The earliest New Testament documents are not the Gospels, but the letters of Paul written to small Christian communities across the Roman Empire. The earliest of these, likely his Letter to the Galatians or perhaps his First Letter to the Thessalonians, was written just twenty years after Jesus' death. In Galatians, Paul describes his own conversion to the Christian faith. His conversion probably occurred within a year or two of Jesus' death; thus in the writings of Paul we're reading the words of a contemporary of Jesus who began to follow Jesus in the 30s, which makes Paul a remarkably early source of testimony about the Christian faith. Paul's association with Christians goes back before his conversion. The Jewish leadership in Jerusalem had given Paul the task of suppressing the fledgling movement of Jesus' followers who claimed that Jesus had risen from the dead. In that role, Paul had authorized the killing of one of the early Christian leaders, a man named Stephen, and had led the effort to arrest others. Shortly afterward, the Jesus whose followers he was persecuting appeared to him in a vision, and the persecutor of the faith became its leading evangelist.

Occasionally a skeptic will try to argue that Jesus could have been a mythical figure, wholly made up by the early church. But the evidence for his existence is overwhelming. Bart Ehrman, professor of religious studies at the University of North Carolina and himself an agnostic, devoted an entire book to examining the historical evidence for the existence of Jesus. He summarized the research this way: "Jesus did exist, whether we like it or not."[2]

My point in mentioning these early documents is not only to affirm that Jesus existed, but to show that we have a number of sources telling us about him and describing what his earliest followers believed about him. In the end, choosing to believe in Jesus is largely about choosing to believe what the earliest Christians taught, preached, and wrote about him.

A Brief Outline of Jesus' Life

Jesus was born sometime before 4 B.C. in the Roman province of Judea, at the time ruled over by Rome's client king, King Herod the Great.* Shortly after Jesus' birth, his family moved to Nazareth in the Galilee region of what was then the Roman province of Syria. Nazareth was a small village, likely comprised of peasants who worked in the nearby city of Sepphoris. Nazareth appears to have been "the other side of the tracks" to the splendor of Sepphoris. We get a sense of the town's dubious reputation when, in John's Gospel, a young man named Philip finds his friend Nathaniel and proclaims that he has met the Messiah, Jesus of Nazareth. To which Nathaniel replies, "Can anything from Nazareth be good?" (John 1:46).

Jesus' parents were Mary and Joseph. Joseph was a woodworker or possibly a stone mason. He may have made

---

* This is the generally accepted date for King Herod's death, and Matthew records that Herod was alive when Jesus was born. The reason Jesus was born at least four years B.C.—before Christ—is that our Gregorian calendars are off by several years.

furniture, repaired agricultural tools, and worked as a handyman. Jesus' parents were devout Jews. Aside from these few facts, we know very little about Jesus' childhood and young adulthood.* The focus of the Gospels is on the final few years of Jesus' life.

Mark, the book that most scholars believe was the earliest of the four Gospels to be written, begins the story of Jesus when he was approximately thirty years old.** At that time Jesus traveled from Nazareth to the Jordan River near Jericho, where his cousin John (known as the Baptizer) was calling the Jewish people to repent of their sins and be immersed in the Jordan as an expression of their penance and desire to turn wholeheartedly to God. The water baptism expressed God's forgiveness of their sins.

Jesus was baptized by his cousin, after which he spent forty days in the desert of Judea, a time recorded as one of testing or temptation. It was undoubtedly also a time in which Jesus, like so many prophets who had gone to the wilderness before him, communed with God and clarified the mission he was about to embark upon. Mark tells us that after returning from the desert, "Jesus came into Galilee announcing God's good news, saying, 'Now is the time! Here comes God's kingdom!

---

* Aside from the stories in Matthew and Luke centered around Jesus' birth and dedication at the Temple, Matthew tells us that Jesus' family fled to Egypt just after his birth, when King Herod the Great sought to kill him. Luke tells us one story from Jesus' youth, when at the age of twelve he was accidentally left in Jerusalem as his family began the journey back to Nazareth following the Passover. They found him after three days in the Temple questioning the priests, a foreshadowing of the way he would question and challenge the religious authorities later in his life. It is notable that even when he was a boy, those who heard him were "amazed" at his questions and conversations with the chief priests.

** It is Luke who tells us Jesus' age when he began his public ministry.

Change your hearts and lives, and trust this good news!'"
(Mark 1:14-15).

Eventually Jesus made the lakeside village of Capernaum
on the Sea of Galilee his home base. He devoted much of the
next three years ministering in the villages around the Sea
of Galilee, with occasional journeys farther afield, including
to Jerusalem and other towns. Matthew summarizes his
ministry with these words:

> *Jesus traveled among all the cities and villages,*
> *teaching in their synagogues, announcing the*
> *good news of the kingdom, and healing every*
> *disease and every sickness. Now when Jesus*
> *saw the crowds, he had compassion for them*
> *because they were troubled and helpless, like*
> *sheep without a shepherd. Then he said to*
> *his disciples, "The size of the harvest is bigger*
> *than you can imagine, but there are few*
> *workers. Therefore, plead with the Lord of the*
> *harvest to send out workers for his harvest."*
> *(Matthew 9:35-38)*

Jesus' ministry was marked by his compassion for the sick,
the marginalized, and those who were "lost." He told stories—
parables—to teach people about God and God's will for their
lives. The widely known phrases "prodigal son" and "good
Samaritan" are taken from two of his most famous parables.
He touched people, he prayed for them, and they were made
well. As a result, many more came to hear Jesus and ask him
to pray for them.

Jesus called ordinary people as his disciples—fishermen, tax collectors, and others, including not only men but a handful of women who also followed him. His best-known ethical teaching is a compilation of things he said on various occasions and is referred to as the Sermon on the Mount. The "Golden Rule," known by nearly everyone, is from the Sermon on the Mount. He summarized God's demands by citing two of Moses's commands: "*You must love the Lord your God with all your heart, with all your being, and with all your mind*" and "*You must love your neighbor as you love yourself*" (Matthew 22:37, 39).

From the outset of his ministry, Jesus found himself at odds with some of the religious authorities. They seemed threatened by the crowds that gathered to hear him. They didn't know what to make of his healings, were at odds with his interpretation of Scripture, and were frustrated by his willingness to violate their rules regarding the Sabbath.

Jesus was also frustrated with many of these religious leaders. He believed they actually pushed people away from God, rather than drawing people to God. He felt some misrepresented God's heart and character and were filled with pride and hypocrisy. We can hear his frustration in words such as these from the Gospel of Matthew:

> *Then Jesus spoke to the crowds and his
> disciples, "The legal experts and the Pharisees
> sit on Moses' seat. Therefore, you must take
> care to do everything they say. But don't do
> what they do. For they tie together heavy
> packs that are impossible to carry. They*

> *put them on the shoulders of others, but*
> *are unwilling to lift a finger to move them.*
> *Everything they do, they do to be noticed by*
> *others. They make extra-wide prayer bands*
> *for their arms and long tassels for their*
> *clothes. They love to sit in places of honor at*
> *banquets and in the synagogues. They love to*
> *be greeted with honor in the markets and to*
> *be addressed as 'Rabbi.'"*
>
> *(Matthew 23:1-7)*

Jesus went on in that same chapter to express warnings to the religious leaders. Here's just one of several warnings he uttered to and about them:

> *"How terrible it will be for you legal experts*
> *and Pharisees! Hypocrites! You are like white-*
> *washed tombs. They look beautiful on the*
> *outside. But inside they are full of dead bones*
> *and all kinds of filth."*
>
> *(Matthew 23:27)*

As you can imagine, Jesus' words and actions set him on a collision course with the religious authorities. The tension reached a breaking point in the third year of his public ministry, when Jesus entered Jerusalem a week before the great festival of Passover. For three years people had been hearing about Jesus and wondering if he might be the long-awaited Messiah. *Messiah* is a Hebrew word that means "anointed one." Its Greek equivalent is *Christ*. Both Messiah and Christ signify that an individual is God's chosen king.

The Hebrew prophets had foretold that God would send a king to rule over his people with justice and righteousness. In the time of Jesus, the Romans occupied the Holy Land, and most Jews longed for the day when Israel would be free of Roman rule and able to live in peace. Jesus saw himself as the fulfillment of this messianic promise, but, as with many other things, he interpreted these Scriptures differently than did the religious leaders and many of the common people.

Jesus was not concerned with overthrowing the Romans. He understood that God's kingdom existed wherever people put their trust in God and sought to love God and love their neighbor. He taught people that the kingdom of God was among them and within them. At Jesus' trial, he told Pontius Pilate that "my kingdom is not of this world" (John 18:36 NKJV). The kingdom that Jesus proclaimed—and this was the central focus of his preaching and teaching, particularly in Matthew, Mark, and Luke—is made up of all who long for God and who seek to do God's will; and this kingdom, though having small beginnings, will eventually transform the temporal kingdoms of this world.

In this kingdom, Jesus proclaimed, people not only love God and their neighbor, they love their enemy. They feed the hungry, clothe the naked, and visit the sick and imprisoned. Citizens of this kingdom practice forgiveness rather than seek revenge. In this kingdom the truly great act as servants, and humility is a cardinal virtue. This is the kingdom Jesus came proclaiming. It is the kingdom he sought to usher in. And yes, he was its King, anointed by God for this role.

As Jesus entered Jerusalem in preparation for the Passover, he asked his disciples to bring him a donkey. There's no evidence that Jesus rode on a donkey any other time, so it's likely he was giving the people a sign. Zechariah the prophet had written, hundreds of years earlier, "Look, your king will come to you. He is righteous and victorious. He is humble and riding on an ass, on a colt, the offspring of a donkey" (Zechariah 9:9).

As Jesus mounted the donkey, the people understood what he was doing. They cut down branches from the trees and began to wave them before him (a traditional sign of victory among the Jewish people). They called out, "*Hosanna* to the Son of David! *Blessings on the one who comes in the name of the Lord! Hosanna* in the highest!" (Matthew 21:9). *Hosanna* is a Hebrew word that was a cry for God's help and deliverance; it literally means "save us now." Shouting this word as Jesus entered the city was, in essence, a prayer that God might use this man, riding on his donkey, to deliver the Jews from the Romans.

Jesus saw the tragic irony in their words. It's why he paused and wept during the celebratory parade. The people sought a leader who would mount a rebellion against Rome. (Others would lead such a rebellion several decades later, a conflict that would end with over a million Jews slaughtered by the Romans, and the city of Jerusalem, with its Temple, destroyed.) The people's hosannas on that Palm Sunday as Jesus entered Jerusalem reflected a desire that Jesus save them from the Romans. What they didn't realize was that Jesus had come to save them, not from the Romans but from themselves.

The enemy he sought to deliver them from was the hate, indifference, pride, and hypocrisy in each human heart—what the Bible calls sin—and the resulting alienation from God and neighbor that sin brings. Further he came to save them from fear, lovelessness, hopelessness, and ultimately, death.

Jesus knew that the journey into Jerusalem would end in his death. In fact, he seemed to view his death as the only way to usher in the kingdom he taught about. On Thursday night of what we now call Holy Week, Jesus had one last meal with his disciples, redefining the meaning of the Jewish Passover Seder. He hoped that his disciples might thereafter share a meal of bread and wine as a means of remembering the events that were about to unfold, while receiving God's grace and communing with him. On Friday morning, at the urging of the religious authorities, the Roman governor Pontius Pilate sentenced Jesus to death by crucifixion for claiming to be a king.

What took place on that "Good" Friday was a divine drama unmasking human evil and demonstrating divine mercy. Jesus was given a crown of thorns as the Roman soldiers mocked him and beat him. He was nailed to a cross, then lifted up to hang before the crowd. They watched as he was left to suffer for six hours before finally expiring. Yet in his death, Christians would come to see profound meaning: an act of divine suffering whose end was redemption for the human race.

He was taken down from the cross and hastily buried in a borrowed tomb. But on Sunday morning, the heavy stone that sealed the entrance to the tomb had been tossed aside, and the tomb was found to be empty. Jesus appeared on that day to a couple of women, and to his disciples and a few others.

Over the next forty days, Jesus appeared again and again to his disciples in various places and ways. Paul notes that Jesus appeared to as many as five hundred people on one occasion, many of whom were still alive when Paul wrote. Finally Jesus bid the disciples farewell one last time and commanded,

> *"Go and make disciples of all nations, baptizing*
> *them in the name of the Father and of the Son*
> *and of the Holy Spirit, teaching them to obey*
> *everything that I've commanded you. Look, I*
> *myself will be with you every day until the end*
> *of this present age."*
>
> *(Matthew 28:19-20)*

There is much I've left out of this outline, and if you are new to the Christian faith or are just searching, I encourage you to read the Gospels for yourself. I suggest starting with Luke. It was in reading the Gospel of Luke that I came to love this man, even before I understood the theological implications of his life.

Let's move from this brief summary of Jesus' life to consider the *meaning* of his life—the things that Christians believe about Jesus and why they matter.

WHAT CHRISTIANS BELIEVE ABOUT JESUS

The question about Jesus isn't whether or not he existed, nor whether he did most of the things I've just described. (Aside from the miracles and the Resurrection, most skeptics would agree that the outline above likely summarizes the events of Jesus' life.) And as we've seen, Jews, Muslims, and even atheists have been willing to view Jesus as a great moral teacher. But Christianity affirms that he is more than a teacher. The New Testament authors saw him as Savior, Christ, or Messiah, and as God's only Son, our Lord.

I'd like to examine some of these titles and names found throughout the New Testament and included in the Apostles' Creed, but first let's consider briefly the Creed's affirmation that Jesus was "conceived by the Holy Spirit" and "born of the Virgin Mary."

Born of the Virgin Mary

For some people, it's simply beyond belief that Mary, the mother of Jesus, conceived Jesus apart from intercourse with a man, by the Holy Spirit's miraculous intervention. I completely understand the skepticism. Not only does it seem biologically impossible, but the idea seems to draw upon ancient stories of children born of unions between women and the gods. Hence even some Christians have set the idea aside as the imaginative work of early Christians seeking to explain how Jesus is "God's only son." These Christians note that only Matthew and Luke in the New Testament include the virgin birth; neither Mark nor John mentions it, nor do Paul and the other New Testament authors. Further, it is noted that

Jesus Christ

Matthew's citation from Isaiah about a virgin conceiving and bearing a son likely meant something very different to Isaiah. Matthew and Luke offer two different accounts of Jesus' birth. Though Matthew and Luke were written in the 70s or 80s, their stories of the virginal conception and birth of Jesus come from an earlier time and circulated independently. Both Gospel authors, writing in different places and for different reasons, know of the virginal conception of Jesus, even if they don't share the same birth stories. (Matthew emphasizes the story from Joseph's vantage point; Luke from Mary's.)

Is it possible to be a Christian and not believe in the virgin birth? Given how little the doctrine is referenced in the New Testament, the answer would clearly seem to be yes. But I wonder if it is really such a hard thing to accept; and, once accepted, if it might offer us some important truths about Jesus.

Scientists today can clone mammals, and who can doubt that one day they will be able to do the same with humans? In nature, we see parthenogenesis—the female of a species conceiving asexually, without fertilization from a male of the species—in certain animals including some species of fish, one species of snake, some lizards, and a variety of insects.[3] In the light of what our scientists can do, and what we see occasionally in nature, a virginal conception of Jesus seems to me not only conceivable but a relatively simple task for God.

And is it possible, in a world where gods were thought to procreate with women, that God might use this very idea, accepted by the pagans, to be the means by which he would bring forth his son? Is it possible that the virginal conception and birth was considered by God to be a beautiful means of expressing deeper mysteries of the Incarnation (which we'll consider in just a moment)? The virginal conception and birth captures in one simple story, with the Spirit's provision of genetic information, something it would take the church three hundred years to explain philosophically—namely, how Jesus was uniquely God's Son, and how God took on human flesh in Jesus Christ.

I once heard a Muslim say that the idea of God's becoming flesh in Jesus, being born in an ordinary way through a woman's birth canal "with blood and bodily fluids," was simply beneath God. But this is part of the story's power and beauty. It was not "beneath" God to get mixed up in our humanity—to be conceived in the womb and born in this messy and very human way; in fact, this is precisely where we see God's glory. God reveals something of God's character in love precisely by coming to us in this humble way.

There is much more that could and should be said about the virginal conception and birth, but at the very least we should mention what Matthew sees in this story. In Matthew 1:23 he notes, quoting Isaiah,

> Look! A virgin will become pregnant and
> give birth to a son,
> And they will call him, *Emmanuel.*

(Emmanuel *means "God with us."*)

In this passage, Matthew tells us why he is including the story. (He could easily have left it on the cutting-room floor, as Mark and John did if they were aware of the story.) The reason is that Matthew understands the virginal conception of Jesus as a way of conveying the deep theological truth that, in Jesus, God has come to be "with us" by becoming one of us—Jesus is Emmanuel.

Jesus: Savior

Now let's look at the various titles and names given Jesus in the Creed, all of which come from the Gospels and the rest of the New Testament. We'll start with the name *Jesus*.

In first-century Judaism most people had one name, followed by a second name that offered another piece of identifying information. The information could be drawn from important relationships, as with John son of Zebedee or Elizabeth wife of Zechariah. You could be identified by your job, as with Levi the Tax Collector; or by your actions, as with John the Baptizer. Or you might be defined by the village you were from, as with Mary from Magdala.

The name Jesus is the Greek form of *Yeshua*, a common name in the first century that is sometimes translated as "deliverer" or "savior." Matthew and Luke tell us that an angel revealed to Mary and Joseph separately that the son Mary would bear was to be named Yeshua. To some he was Yeshua ben Yosef (Jesus son of Joseph). To some he was Yeshua the Carpenter. To some he was Yeshua of Nazareth.

If we take Matthew and Luke at face value, it was God who wanted this child to receive the name Yeshua. His name was a sign of what he would do. The angel told Joseph, "You will call him Jesus, because he will save his people from their sins" (Matthew 1:21).

If Jesus came to save us from sin, it is important to consider what is meant by the word *sin*. Some don't like the word—it sounds antiquated or judgmental or repressive. But the concept in Scripture is actually a helpful one.

The Greek word for sin used most often in the New Testament is *hamartia*, and it means "to miss the mark." This word points to the fact that there is a "mark" we're meant to hit—a path we're meant to follow, a way we're meant to live. Most of us get this. We're meant to be loving, compassionate, just, merciful, giving, honest. As Jesus expressed it, we're created with two overriding aims in life: to love God with all that is within us and to love our neighbor as we love ourselves. So sin is anything we do in thought, word, or deed that is inconsistent with loving God or neighbor.

Who wouldn't agree that most of the world's pain is because people and societies miss the mark or stray from the right path—because they fail to practice love? The evening news bears witness to the fact that human beings struggle with sin, and that this sin has tragic consequences. I think of mass shootings that have become a part of the world we live in, as have the steady stream of government scandals around the world and the dictatorial rulers who oppress their own people. Proof of the human struggle with *hamartia*—missing the mark—is readily available to any who observe humanity.

All the world's wars, violence, poverty, and injustice fall into this category. So do the things we say and do each day to hurt one another. And which of us has not at times failed to say or do something we should have done to help someone else? From the inhumanity we see on a macro scale, to the selfishness and self-centeredness at work in our own hearts, it is clear that sin is a fundamental part of the human condition. If Jesus was born to save us from our sins, he clearly has a huge mission.

His saving us from our sins is not just about forgiving our sins or, as we often hear, dying for our sins. Of course Jesus offers forgiveness, redemption, and mercy to those who repent and seek it. And yes, this forgiveness gives us right standing with God (we'll focus on forgiveness in a later chapter). But saving humanity from our sins involves far more than forgiveness; it means affecting those of us who believe in him so deeply that we are changed. It involves a spiritual transformation that shows us a better way and gives us the ability to pursue it.

I don't merely want to be forgiven over and over again. I want to hit the mark. I want to be a loving, compassionate, merciful human being who does the right thing more often than not. I don't want to be blind to the ways I hurt others; I want to see them for what they are and find the strength to act differently.

Jesus came to save us from our sins—to deliver us from the power and lure of sin. He does this by showing us God, by calling us to follow him, by modeling what it means to be authentically human, by demonstrating selfless sacrificial love, and by working to change our hearts—God's work in us that is usually described by the words *conversion* and *sanctification*. He seeks to reorient our lives from the inside out, and in so doing to save us from being self-centered, self-absorbed, narcissistic creatures and to make us people who truly do love God and neighbor.

I continue to miss the mark. It's embarrassing to see how many times in a week I blow it. It's discouraging and disappointing. But for every time I've missed the mark, there are several times when I think I may have hit it—times when I sought to do what is right, not for recognition or some self-serving reason but because my heart, values, and decisions have changed over time as I sought to follow Jesus.

In looking across human history, our need to be saved seems self-evident to me. In the twentieth century alone, as humanity became more technologically advanced, we killed more human beings than ever before by acts of war, neglect, and oppression. In the twenty-first century, the gap between rich and poor continues to widen within each country and between the developed and the developing countries. We face mental health problems in America. We struggle with moral crises at the individual level. And then of course there is our relentless effort to postpone death that leads to exorbitant health-care costs, particularly as we try to eke out a few more months or even days from our lives. This latter reflects our fundamental fear of death.

We need to be saved. Jesus Christ came to be our Savior, to deliver us. He is God's response to the human condition, God's answer to the questions we wrestle with and the struggles we face. John's Gospel begins by referring to Jesus as "the Word made flesh." Jesus incarnates God's Word to us. This Word has power. It is a message about God and about humanity that was wrapped in a person, Jesus Christ. It is a Word that at one and the same time diagnoses our problem and provides the solution. In his life, death, and resurrection, Jesus revealed who God is and who we are; he revealed our sin and God's suffering in order to deliver us from it; and he demonstrated and embodied the redemptive love of God and his infinite mercy.

I would offer one more comment here about Jesus' saving work. Often this work is spoken of as Christ's atoning work. *Atonement* is an old English word that was created to try to express the meaning of other words in Greek and Hebrew. It captures the sense of "at-one-ment" with God—in other words, the act of atonement reconciles us to God.

There are many theories of the atonement—ideas about how Jesus' life, death, and resurrection reconcile us to God. Entire books have been devoted to this topic. I find it interesting that none of the Christian creeds offers a particular theory of atonement as *the* right view of how Jesus' death atones for human sin. The Apostles' Creed, for example, only notes that Jesus was crucified, dead, and buried but mentions nothing about atonement. The Nicene Creed states that Jesus was "crucified for us" but goes no farther in explaining precisely how his death brings about our at-one-ment with God.

The question of how Christ's death "saves" us is perplexing to many people, Christians and non-Christians alike. We Christians believe it and usually can give a superficial explanation, but when pressed, our explanations just seem to raise more questions. A nominally religious man I know recently said:

> I guess I'm not smart enough or spiritual enough to understand Jesus' death on the cross. When my kids mess up, I sometimes get angry but mostly I just feel

disappointed. But Christianity seems to teach that God not only gets angry, but that he has to punish sin in order to forgive. That doesn't make any sense to me. Aren't we supposed to forgive others without seeking retribution? Why then does God require punishment to forgive? Christians teach that God is so loving that he sends Jesus, but then God tortures the hell out of him to work out his anger against human sin? That sounds like child abuse. Does God really need Jesus to be tortured to death to forgive sins? That just seems messed up to me!

This man had drawn his understanding about the Christian view of atonement from a particular theory called Penal Substitutionary Atonement. *Penal* means "punishment." *Substitutionary* signifies that Jesus served as a substitute, taking the punishment the human race deserved. The way this often sounds to non-Christians (as well as to many Christians) is very much the way the man I just described had heard it.

There are three ideas that I think are helpful in thinking about atonement. The first is the idea I mentioned above, that the New Testament offers multiple analogies for the ways in which Jesus' death on the cross brings about our salvation. The operative word here is *analogies*. An analogy is a likening of one thing that is less easily understood to a second thing that is more easily understood. The meaning of Jesus' death and how it saves us is understood in the New Testament using various analogies, not just one. In the New Testament his death is an expression of his love for others, an offering to God, a payment made to purchase a slave's freedom, a Passover lamb that delivers from death, an exemplar for human living, an act of penal substitution suffered for the sins of others.

As I think about these different analogies, it's clear that each breaks down when pushed too far. Nevertheless, each analogy reveals a different and helpful way of describing some dimension of Jesus' atoning work. Some of the analogies may speak to us more profoundly than others at any given time in our lives. At times, for example, I most need to know that Jesus' death demonstrates the depth of divine love for me. At other times I need to know that Jesus purchased me on the cross and that grace is not cheap. Sometimes I need to know that the punishment I deserve for a sin has instead been suffered by him and for me. There are moments I look at the cross and see the glory of his self-giving and his call for me to live selflessly. No one analogy encompasses the entirety of the meaning of Christ's death.

This leads to a second idea I've found helpful in teaching about the atonement. The atonement is not so much like math, economics, or even law; it's not a formula or something that mechanistically works. Instead it is far more like poetry, drama, sculpture, or some other form of art. Walking through one of the world's finest art museums I've stumbled upon a masterpiece here or there that stopped me in my tracks. These were works where the artist was clearly seeking to *speak*—commenting on the times, interpreting some event, or calling for a response from the viewer. These pieces have moved me, spoken to me, and led me to deeper insights or ideas. Music, poetry, and theater, at their best, do the same.

In Jesus' death and resurrection, a divine drama unfolds, a masterpiece is seen, a concerto is heard that leaves those who ponder it speechless and moved to the depths of their souls. It is intended to move the one hearing or viewing the cross to repentance, to an awareness of God's redeeming love, grace, and mercy. If a picture is worth a thousand words, then the image of Jesus' suffering and death on the cross speaks a message that has the power to redeem the world.

The third idea I've found helpful is this: God did not need Jesus to suffer and die on the cross in order to save us. Rather, *we* needed it, so we could know the depth of human sin, the breadth of God's graciousness and love, and ultimately God's triumph over sin and death. Jesus did suffer and die for our sins—not because God insisted on torturing his son in order to satisfy or appease his wrath, but because by this dramatic act God hoped to finally break though to us, to affect and change us, to save us from our sin and alienation from God.

A couple I know found their marriage nearly destroyed by the husband's affair. The woman came to our sanctuary and touched the cross, and as she did she wept. In that moment, the cross was a sign for her that Christ knew the rejection she was feeling and a sign of the depth of God's love for her. That week, her husband came to that same cross, embraced it, and wept, because for him the cross was a sign that Christ had borne his sin and that, despite the mess he'd made of his life, he could be forgiven—if not by his wife, at least by God. The "old rugged cross" is a dramatic, divine word to humanity, a word that has the power to reconcile us to God, to make us at-one-with him.

Christ: Messiah

The Creed also refers to Jesus as the "Christ." You know, of course, that Christ is not Jesus' last name, but instead, as we learned earlier, a title describing a particular role he came to play. Again, Christ is from the Greek word for "anointed one," the word drawn from the Hebrew that has the same meaning as Messiah.

Part of the ancient coronation ceremony by which an individual became king over the people of God was having a particular preparation of oil poured or smeared on one's head by the high priest. This act signified that the individual was set apart for God's purposes and belonged to God. It also signified that the person was chosen by God to reign on God's behalf.

I was surprised to learn recently that as far back as anyone can remember, the kings and queens of England are also anointed at their coronation. I visited the Tower of London a couple of years ago and toured the display where the crown jewels are held. There I watched a video from June 2, 1953, showing the coronation of Queen Elizabeth II. The oil was poured from an ampulla onto a spoon. Then the Archbishop of Canterbury placed his thumb in the oil and smeared it on the queen's hands, then just below her neck, and then on her head in the sign of the cross—consecrating her hands, her heart, and her mind to ruling on God's behalf.

The term "Christ" or "Messiah" could be used in ancient times by any king chosen by God to rule over God's people. Christians claim Jesus as their King. They give him their highest allegiance. He is our Christ, our Messiah.

Each day when I wake up, I slip to my knees to pray and offer my life once more in his service. I invite him to lead and guide me and to use me to do whatever he wills. As I think about Jesus as the Christ, and how this commitment affects my daily life, I'm reminded of the famous words in President Kennedy's 1961 inaugural address: "Ask not what your country can do for you, ask what you can do for your country." That's how I see my commitment to Jesus as the Christ. I don't ask each day what he will do for me, but what he would have me do in service to him and his kingdom.

God's Only Son, Our Lord

The Creed goes on to identify faith in Jesus, who is "his [God's] only Son, our Lord." The Bible teaches that human beings are God's sons and daughters. So what does the Creed mean by affirming that Jesus is God's *only* Son? To speak of Jesus in this way is to speak of a special and unique relationship that Jesus has with God. Jesus is not just *a* son of God, but *the* Son of God.

Before exploring the meaning of this phrase, I would remind you that all human language is symbolic; sounds, letters, and words all represent something else. Words cannot fully contain the thing they are meant to represent but can only approximate a deeper reality.

Take a simple example: the color blue. When I say that something is blue, what does that mean? We might first need to clarify what we mean by blue, since there are thousands of shades of blue. Is it sky blue, navy blue, royal blue, baby blue? Once we clarify the precise shade of blue we're speaking of, we'd need to ask what we mean when we say a thing *is* blue. Physicists tell us that a blue object is not inherently blue; instead, its chemical properties reflect those wavelengths of light that are in the blue part of the spectrum. Our eyes "see" this reflected light, and our brain tells us the object is blue.

Here's the point: saying that Jesus is "God's only Son" is shorthand for something much deeper. The phrase will ultimately take us to the doctrine of the divinity of Jesus. But initially, let's consider how Jesus' first followers saw him.

When Jesus called his first disciples, they felt compelled to leave whatever they were doing and to follow him. They did not understand him to be the only Son of God, but they did feel drawn to him. When Jesus taught, he taught with an authority the other religious leaders did not demonstrate, and soon large crowds were drawn to him. When Jesus spoke, many people felt they had heard the very words of God. When Jesus touched people, they felt they had been touched by God. When they answered his call, they felt they were answering God's call.

In addition, Jesus did things that ordinary people could not do. He ministered to the mentally ill and demon-possessed, and he sent the demons and mental illnesses to flight. He healed the sick and opened the eyes of the blind. He commanded the storms on the Sea of Galilee to be still, and they stopped instantly. He was even reported to have raised the dead.

Skeptics dismiss the miracles as stories fabricated by early Christians to win followers to Jesus. But believers view them as actual historical events and as signs that point to the unique identity of Jesus. I love the words of the disciples in Mark 4:41. Jesus had just calmed the winds and the waves in the midst of a violent storm on the Sea of Galilee. The disciples were "overcome with awe," and they asked one another, "Who then is this? Even the wind and the sea obey him!"

Indeed, who *is* this? So much of what Jesus did were things that, according to Scripture, only God could do, be it forgiving sins, raising the dead, or commanding the winds and waves. Seeing Jesus do these things, early Christians came to believe that in some sense God had come to the human race in the person of Jesus. The theological term for this is "incarnation," a term that means, literally, to enflesh. Christians believe that God took on flesh and came to us in Jesus.

James Stewart, one of the great preachers of twentieth-century Scotland, was a prolific writer and later professor of New Testament in Edinburgh. He captured well the significance of the Gospels' healing and miracle stories when he wrote,

> It is a tragedy that the Christian religion is in many
> minds identified merely with pious ethical behavior
> and vague theistic beliefs, suffused with aesthetic
> emotionalism and a mild glow of humanitarian
> benevolence. This is not the faith which first awakened
> the world like a thousand trumpets and made people
> feel it bliss in such a dawn to be alive. Men knew what
> Christianity really was—the entrance into history of a
> force of immeasurable range.[4]

Calming the violent storms, casting out demons, making the lame to walk and the blind to see, even raising the dead—

it's easy to understand how skeptics could question whether these things really happened. But if Jesus of Nazareth was more than a man, if in fact God had come to us in him, walking on our planet, would these acts not be the very kinds of things we would expect as he encountered suffering, darkness, and death?

As I think about the idea of incarnation—of God coming to us in human flesh—I'm reminded of the 1995 hit song, "One of Us." In it, singer Joan Osborne asks what it would be like if God was "a slob like one of us." This is not far from what Christians profess as it relates to Jesus.

But how, precisely, was Jesus God? Did God only seem to be human in Jesus, the way God took on the appearance of George Burns, a kind elderly man in the 1977 film *Oh, God!* or of Morgan Freeman in the 2003 film *Bruce Almighty*? The mainstream of Christian faith has rejected this idea, saying that God did not merely appear in human form, but that in Jesus, God truly entered into our humanity—Jesus was fully human. But then how was he also God? Did God descend upon him at baptism? Or was he filled with the Spirit, as happened with the Hebrew prophets? Or was Jesus both somehow God and human from his birth? And if the latter, how is this even possible?

If you struggle to explain or make sense of the Incarnation or the deity of Christ, you are in good company. The church wrestled with these questions for nearly three hundred years until finally, at the Council of Nicaea in 325, they settled on language clarifying what the majority of the church believed.

There, in the Nicene Creed, the Council affirmed that Jesus Christ was

> God from God, Light from Light,
> true God from true God,
> begotten, not made,
> of one Being with the Father.[5]

Even so, continued clarification and wordsmithing would take place in 381 at a council in Constantinople, in 431 at the Third Ecumenical Council at Ephesus, and again in 451 at the Council of Chalcedon.* But it is important to note that while the church's "orthodox" beliefs about the divinity of Christ were codified in these councils, the seeds of these views are found in the earliest documents of the Christian faith.

Some critics like to suggest that it wasn't until the fourth century that the church "transformed" Jesus from a simple rabbi to a divine figure. But consider Paul's Letter to the Philippians, written in the early 60s. In it, Paul quotes an early Christian hymn that predates his letter. Note what this hymn of the early church said about Jesus:

> *Though he was in the form of God,*
>   *he did not consider being equal with God*
>   *something to exploit.*
> *But he emptied himself*
>   *by taking the form of a slave*
>   *and by becoming like human beings.*

---

* In the appendix of this book, you'll find the texts of several major Christian creeds, including the original Nicene Creed, the Nicene Creed as modified at Constantinople, the Chalcedonian Creed, and the Athanasian Creed.

> *When he found himself in the form of a human,*
> *he humbled himself by becoming obedient*
> *to the point of death,*
> *even death on a cross.*
>
> *(Philippians 2:6-8)*

These words were quoted by Paul some 270 years before the Council of Nicea drafted its creed affirming that Jesus was both God and human. Similarly, consider the words to another first-century hymn, found in Paul's Letter to the Colossians:

> *The Son is the image of the invisible God,*
> *the one who is first over all creation,*
>
> *Because all things were created by him:*
> *both in the heavens and on the earth,*
> *the things that are visible and the things*
> *that are invisible.*
> *Whether they are thrones or powers,*
> *or rulers or authorities,*
> *all things were created through him and for him.*
>
> *He existed before all things,*
> *and all things are held together in him.*
>
> *(Colossians 1:15-17)**

---

* Many mainline scholars believe that Colossians was written after Paul's death by one of his associates, drawing upon his message. In either case, however, it is typically dated to the first century.

These hymns show that very early on, the church was coming to understand that something of the man Jesus was "in the form of God" and that somehow the Son of God was Son of God before he became flesh in Jesus Christ.

Here it might be a good time to bring in the word *Lord*. This is the most frequently used title for Jesus in the New Testament. It appears 537 times in the New Testament. In Greek the word is *Kyrios* or *Kurios*, and it means master, ruler, or sovereign, and it can also mean king. The term signified the highest authority in a particular span of control. In the patriarchal society of ancient times, the husband or father was typically the lord of the house. The leader of a city was lord of the city. The king was lord of his kingdom. The title was used of Augustus Caesar, who was lord of lords, signifying the highest authority in the empire.

When the Old Testament was being translated from Hebrew to Greek and the translators were trying to find the right Greek word for the holy proper name frequently used of God in the Old Testament—Yahweh—they settled on the Greek word *Kyrios*, or Lord. So when Christians in the New Testament, beginning with the earliest document in the New Testament, speak of Jesus, the title they most frequently use for him is Lord; and they don't refer to Jesus as *a* lord, but *the* Lord, the same title used for God's proper name throughout the earliest Greek translation of the Old Testament.

The point of all this is to emphasize that—in contrast to the claims of some critics—Christians from the earliest times were, in some not-fully-defined way, associating Jesus with God. But if Jesus' identity wasn't clearly defined in most of the New Testament, John sought to bring greater clarity when he wrote his Gospel. Listen to the dramatic prologue to the Gospel of John,

> *In the beginning was the Word*
> *and the Word was with God*
> *and the Word was God.*
> *The Word was with God in the beginning.*
> *Everything came into being through the Word,*
> *and without the Word*
> *nothing came into being.*
> *What came into being*
> *through the Word was life,*
> *and the life was the light for all people.*
> *The light shines in the darkness,*
> *and the darkness doesn't extinguish the*
> *light....*
>
> *The Word became flesh*
> *and made his home among us.*
> *We have seen his glory,*
> *glory like that of a father's only son,*
> *full of grace and truth.*
>
> *(John 1:1-5, 14)*

The Greek term translated as *Word* in this prologue is *logos*, from which the English word *logic* derives (as well as every English word ending in *-ology*). *Logos* is the mind, the logic, the creative power, the reasoning, and even the character and power of God. *Logos* as used here also represents God's desire to reveal himself to humanity—to speak to the human race. From this Word all things were created. Without it, nothing came into being. A full 235 years before the Council of Nicea, John affirms, "The Word became flesh and made his home among us," and "the Word was with God and the Word was God."

Jesus is the divine Word that reveals the depth of God's love. He describes and demonstrates God's concern for the marginalized, the outcast, and the sinner. He speaks of God's compassion and mercy. He decisively bears humanity's sin and then defeats death in his resurrection.

John regularly points to the idea that Jesus somehow embodies God's divine essence. We hear it in Jesus' repeated use of "I Am" statements.* (As we saw in the previous chapter, I Am was the name by which God revealed himself to Moses, signifying that God is the source of being or existence itself.) We hear it when Jesus says, "I and the Father are one" (John 10:30) and "Whoever has seen me has seen the Father" (John 14:9). We see it in the way Jesus repeatedly does things we would expect only God could do. And we see it near the end of John's Gospel when, after the Resurrection, Thomas encounters the resurrected Jesus and cries out, "My Lord and my God!" (John 20:28).

What a remarkable idea—that the God who rules the universe would come to us, like one of us, born to a peasant family with an animals' feeding trough as his first bed; that he would choose to experience what it means to be human;

---

* See John 6:20; 8:24, 28, 58; 13:19; 18:5, 6, and 8 as well as the multiple "I Am" sayings that are likely intended to draw upon this same theme.

that he would know joy and sorrow, love and hate, pain and death. He ate, he wept, he bled, and he died. In Jesus, surely God experienced our humanity. But the Incarnation was not simply to have God walk in our shoes; it was to allow God, literally, to meet us on our own ground—to become one of us in order to reveal himself to us in terms that we could understand, showing us what he is like and what his will is for our lives and for the world.

Still, questions remain. How exactly did divinity and humanity meet in Jesus? If we could have examined Jesus with the help of an MRI scan, would we have seen anything different from an ordinary man? The fourth- and fifth-century creeds use technical theological language to explain how humanity and divinity were brought together in Jesus, but we're still left with a mystery.

Christian doctrine, the kind of thing I'm writing about throughout this book, is important. It matters. But I believe our discussions of these mysteries should reflect what some have called a "generous orthodoxy"—an approach that includes a graciousness and humility toward others who don't express the faith in precisely the same way we do. Our theology is not right theology if it does not lead us to love and mercy and grace.*

---

* Tragically, in the history of Christian thought there were times when these creedal formulations were used to anathematize or demonize followers of Jesus who did not use precisely the same wording formulated by the creeds. It is worth noting that Jesus did not feel compelled to explain the Incarnation to his followers, nor to articulate the finer points of what become Christian orthodoxy. Instead he simply invited people to follow him.

In this chapter we've summarized Jesus' life. We've spoken of some terms used to describe Jesus. We've looked at the meaning of his death and how we make sense of his divinity. I'd like to end this chapter by examining two of the remaining phrases in the section on Jesus in the Apostles' Creed: "he descended to the dead," and "On the third day he rose again."

Descended to the Dead

There are two versions of the Apostles' Creed that are used in churches today. In The United Methodist Church, of which I am a part, we tend to leave out the line that says Jesus "descended to the dead," which is sometimes written "descended to hell" or "descended to Hades." Whatever the wording, the phrase is interesting enough that I'd like to mention a few words about it.

This phrase is the early church's answer to this question: what was Jesus up to between the time of his death on Friday afternoon and his resurrection early Sunday morning? It also points to the early church's understanding of what happens to us when we die.

The Jews had long believed that at death, one's soul made its abode in the realm of the dead. This realm of the dead was also called Sheol or Hades, and it was understood to be under the earth. Within this underworld were two realms— one for the righteous, called Paradise; and another for the unrighteous, often referred to as Gehenna, after the valley in Jerusalem where the city's refuse was burned.

Jesus once told a parable about a poor beggar named Lazarus who sat outside the gates of a certain rich man. The rich man refused to help Lazarus. After they both died, the rich man was in Gehenna, in torment, from which place he looked across a wide chasm and saw Lazarus in the bosom of Abraham —in Paradise. Jesus' parable was rooted in the Jewish belief about the two realms in the place of the dead. Also, you may recall that on the cross Jesus turned to one of the thieves and said, "Today you will be with me in paradise" (Luke 23:43). Paradise was not heaven but the place in the underworld where the righteous dead were comforted awaiting the final resurrection. It was heaven-like but incomplete.

The dead awaited the final judgment. They were spirits, alive and experiencing either blessings or curses, but they were not yet clothed in their new or heavenly bodies. Likewise they were not yet in heaven but were "shades" living in the "shadowlands."

When the Creed says that Jesus "descended to the dead," the idea is that Jesus experienced what we experience when we die. But there was more than just his experiencing the realm of the dead. The church also came to believe that Jesus, during the time between his death and resurrection, offered salvation to those in death's clutches since the beginning of the world. Jesus' actions during that time are referred to as the "harrowing of hell." This triumphant event is often captured in icons that show Jesus tearing the gates of hell off their hinges in order to release the righteous dead from Sheol or Hades. He is often portrayed holding Adam and Eve by the wrist and pulling them out of hell and to heaven.

Though the phrase "descended to the dead" represents speculative theology about which we have limited data in

Scripture, I think there is great power in the image of Christ descending to the realm of the dead, tearing the doors off their hinges, and offering salvation and life to those who had died from the beginning of the human race up until his time. In this image, Christ is seen as triumphantly defeating death itself in keeping with his words, "I have the keys of Death and the Grave" (Revelation 1:18).

On the Third Day...

Virtually no one doubts that Jesus was crucified under Pontius Pilate sometime around A.D. 30. Likewise, it's widely accepted that he was hastily buried in a borrowed tomb and that a large stone was rolled over the mouth of the tomb. The Gospel accounts are consistent with first-century burial practices and one can see such tombs from the period when visiting Israel today. But the earliest Christians made an outrageous claim as to what happened next. They said that early on Sunday morning, roughly thirty-six hours after he was buried, some of the women who followed Jesus returned to the tomb.* The stone had been rolled away and the grave was open. His body was gone.

Soon Jesus began appearing to his disciples and others. They did not always recognize him at first. When Mary Magdalene first saw him she thought he was the gardener. When Cleopas and another follower of Jesus met him that day he appeared

---

* I'm often asked why the Apostles' Creed says that Jesus was raised on the third day when only thirty-six hours had passed. The answer is that Jews counted days from sunset to sunset. On Friday afternoon Jesus died and was buried before sunset; this was counted as the first day. Friday night and all day Saturday were the second day. Saturday night and all day Sunday were the third day. Jesus thus rose "on the third day."

simply as a stranger, as he did another day when his disciples saw him on the shoreline of the Sea of Galilee. For forty days he appeared to them in various times and places before the appearances stopped. As noted earlier, it was Paul who gave us our earliest written account of the Resurrection. He noted that, in all, Jesus appeared to more than five hundred people, most of whom were still alive when Paul wrote his First Letter to the Corinthians. Paul himself claimed to have seen the risen Lord in a vision and heard him speak; it was this vision that led to Paul's dramatic conversion from persecutor of Christians to its leading evangelist.

The resurrection of Jesus is a difficult thing for people to believe. Some critical Christian scholars have suggested that Jesus wasn't literally raised from the dead, but that his followers believed he was with God in heaven and they recognized that he lived on in their hearts and minds and through their continuation of his work. Perhaps, some suggest, a few of these disciples may even have had visions of him after his death.

Yet the disciples and the early church did not simply proclaim that Jesus was dead and lived on in heaven and in their hearts; rather, they pointed to an empty tomb and noted that Jesus' body was gone. Further, they claimed not only to have seen him but to have touched him and eaten with him at various times during a period of several weeks. The disciples were radically changed by their experiences with Jesus following his resurrection. These men, who had fled when Jesus was arrested and had been hiding behind locked doors the day after his death, became bold and courageous, risking their own lives to proclaim what they had seen.

It was the witness of these disciples, along with the empty tomb, that led hundreds and then thousands in Jerusalem to believe. Those who came to believe in the risen Jesus found their own lives changed by their faith, and many of them had their own personal spiritual encounters with him, which led them to accept that he indeed was with them always, even to the end of the age.

In my own life, when I first read the account of Jesus' resurrection in Matthew's Gospel, I found it unbelievable. I next studied Mark's Gospel, and when I read of the empty tomb, once more I was skeptical. It was only when I came to the end of Luke's Gospel that finally I believed. As we noted earlier, believing is a choice. I chose to believe that Jesus rose. Why? I suppose at some level I decided to trust the first disciples, whose accounts were captured in the Gospels. As with the virginal conception and the miracles of Jesus, it seemed to me that the God who commanded "Let there be light!" could do whatever was necessary to transform or reanimate the corpse of Jesus, raising him from the dead.

But more than that, at some level the Resurrection simply came to make sense theologically. If Jesus had come from God to re-present and reveal God and God's will to humanity, and if in some way Jesus was God's response to the existential questions and struggles we face, then his resurrection not only made sense, it was absolutely essential. If Christ was not raised, then evil, hate, sin, and death had the final word on that Friday when Jesus was crucified. But Jesus' resurrection was God's dramatic way of making clear that none of these things really have the final word.

It seemed to me, then and now, that Jesus' resurrection was not only God's response to human mortality and our fear of death, but God's response to all that is wrong in the world. It's an ever-present sign of God's victory and the triumph of good over evil, love over hate, and life over death. Faith in the resurrection of Jesus Christ changes how we live our lives and how we face death, our own and that of others. The Resurrection is so central to our faith that if Jesus' life had ended with his burial, I don't believe Christianity would exist today.

WHY FAITH IN JESUS MATTERS

Some years ago, a rabbi friend invited me to observe the Passover Seder with her family. She said the story that is retold and reenacted in the Passover Seder is the Jewish people's defining story. She noted, "We once were slaves. God heard our cry, had compassion upon us, delivered us, and made us his people. If you are a Jew, you've got to get this story. It is our defining story."

This is how Christians see the story of Jesus. It's our defining story. Jesus demonstrates who God is, what God is like, and what God's will is for our lives. His life and ministry, his death and resurrection shape how we see ourselves and how we see the world.

Ingmar Bergman once said, "You were born without purpose, you live without meaning, living is its own meaning. When you die, you are extinguished. From being you will be transformed to non-being." But faith in Jesus offers a very different perspective. We were born with purpose, our lives have meaning, and when this mortal body dies, we've only just begun to live.

Richard Dawkins once famously wrote, "We are survival machines—robot vehicles blindly programmed to preserve the selfish molecules know as genes."[6] But faith in Jesus says that we were made for more than this. In fact, the pain and brokenness in our world are largely the result of our living as "robot vehicles" blindly focused on serving the self. Jesus calls us to be authentically human, to love, give, serve, and rise above our selfish genes. As we do so, we not only make the world a more just and compassionate place; we find joy in the process.

Yale historian Jaroslav Pelikan captured well the impact Jesus has had on the world. He wrote, "Regardless of what anyone may personally think or believe about him, Jesus of Nazareth has been the dominant figure in the history of Western culture for almost twenty centuries. If it were possible, with some sort of super magnet, to pull up out of the history every scrap of metal bearing at least a trace of his name, how much would be left?"[7]

For Father's Day last year, my then twenty-five-year-old daughter Rebecca, who is living in New York, sent me a gift. I was getting ready for church and the doorbell rang. And there was a delivery person with a balloon, a card, and a container with beautiful plants. I opened the card and read it: "Dad, Happy Father's Day. You are my hero and I am so proud to call you my Dad. Rebecca." I put this miniature garden of succulents on my desk, and every time I look at them I am reminded that I'm loved by my daughter.

When God sought to communicate his love for us, he sent Jesus. It was in his Son that God's message, God's Word, came to us and became our defining story. Through Jesus, God was saying: I Am. You matter to me. I love you.

In Jesus, God showed that he cares about those who are lost and those who are made to feel small. He showed us compassion for the sick. He showed us how to love, to forgive, to give, to serve. In Jesus' death on the cross, God showed us the depth of his love and the costliness of grace. And in Jesus' resurrection, God defeated evil, hate, sin, and death.

We've covered a lot of ground in this chapter. We've explored mysteries that our minds are inadequate to comprehend fully. In writing these words, I'm reminded of Karl Barth, the great twentieth-century theologian, who devoted fourteen volumes to expressing the truths I'm trying to cover in this one short book. Yet despite those fourteen volumes, when Barth was asked by a student if he could summarize in one sentence his theological work, Barth responded by reciting the words of a song his mother had taught him as a child: "Jesus loves me, this I know, for the Bible tells me so."[8]

Yes, Jesus loves me. Jesus loves you, too. And that makes all the difference.

3.

THE HOLY SPIRIT

I believe in the Holy Spirit...

We come now to the Christian confession of faith in the Holy Spirit. After studying the Creed's many statements about Jesus, the single line about the Holy Spirit feels imbalanced and almost anemic: "I believe in the Holy Spirit." But, as we will see, this is the most understated line in the Creed.

You may rightly point out that the Holy Spirit has already been mentioned in the Creed, which includes the previous statement that Jesus "was conceived by the Holy Spirit." Because of that line, you could say that everything stated about Jesus in the Creed is possible because of the Spirit's work. You might also say that everything that follows the confession of belief in the Holy Spirit—the church, forgiveness, the Resurrection—is made possible by the Spirit's work.

In this chapter we'll consider who the Holy Spirit is, what the Holy Spirit does, and why the Holy Spirit matters.

THE VOICES THAT INFLUENCE AND SHAPE US

Before delving into what the Bible says about the Holy Spirit, I'd like us to think together about the voices we hear in our heads, and the forces that shape and influence our lives. We all have voices we hear in our heads or deep down in our hearts—some good voices, some not so good. Sometimes we hear old tapes from childhood, such as a parent telling us that we're "stupid" or "worthless" or "bad." Sometimes we hear voices telling us there's no reason to keep living, or that we'll always feel as depressed as we feel right now. Sometimes the voices remind us of hurts others have inflicted upon us, thus encouraging us to continue on a path of bitterness and resentment. Sometimes the voices are like the mesmerizing song of the sirens in Greek mythology, luring the sailors to run their ships aground; for us, the song might be the whisper of the tempter calling us to do things that enslave and destroy us.

Of course, there are actual human voices we listen to in life as well. Some of these voices influence us positively, making us more loving, compassionate, and kind. Others influence us to harden our hearts and to do things we should never do. I think of the radio broadcasts in Rwanda in 1993 and 1994 on the RTLMC station that fueled racial violence and contributed to the genocide that left 800,000 Tutsi and moderate Hutu dead, and many wounded.* How many times throughout human history have there been voices of political

---

* Radio Télévision Libre des Mille Collines made broadcasts from July 8, 1993, to July 31, 1994, and is widely believed to have played a critical role in inciting some Hutu people to kill their Tutsi and moderate Hutu neighbors.

leaders or parties that led populations to enslave or murder entire people groups?

Among the positive voices we hear are those that lead us to be more authentically human; they call us to love, inspire us to serve, and challenge us to be more than we otherwise would be. These voices help us to know that our lives matter and that we are valued and loved. Loving parents and grandparents provide these voices. The best leaders in religion, politics, and business do the same.

What voices do you listen to? Do these voices—friends, media, politicians, even preachers—lead you to become more like the person God wants you to be, or less? How are the voices shaping your soul? The Apostle Paul speaks of "spiritual warfare," the battle that goes on for our hearts and minds. I love how the opening story in the Bible captures this battle in terms of voices that we hear. The story describes God's command to Adam and Eve to refrain from eating the forbidden fruit. But then a conversation with the serpent in Eden ensues, and they choose to listen to the serpent and eat what God had explicitly taught them to leave alone. Today the tempter continues to whisper in our ears, daily for most of us, beckoning us to do the very things that will bring harm to others or to ourselves.

When we speak about the Holy Spirit, or the Spirit of God, we are speaking of God's active work in our lives; of God's way of leading us, guiding us, forming and shaping us; of God's power and presence to comfort and encourage us and to make us the people God wants us to be. The Spirit is the voice of God whispering, wooing, and beckoning us. And in listening to *this* voice and being shaped by *this* power, we find that we become most fully and authentically human.

The word *spirit* shows up about five hundred times in the Bible. In the Old Testament the Hebrew word usually translated as "spirit" is *ruach*. In the New Testament the Greek word is *pneuma*. The words have multiple meanings including breath, air, wind, and of course spirit. Our word *pneumatic* comes from this Greek word, for example, and is used to describe anything that is powered by air, including pipe organs, air brakes, and industrial machinery that works on compressed air, just to name a few.

When translators find the words *ruach* or *pneuma* in the Old and New Testament, they have to decide based upon the context whether the author meant wind, breath, or spirit, and if it is spirit, whether the word should be capitalized, signifying that it refers to God's Spirit, or whether it remains lowercased, signifying that it refers to the human spirit or some other kind of spirit.

You can see how different translators interpret these words in the opening verses of the Bible. The New Revised Standard Version translates the Hebrew of Genesis 1:1-2 in this way:

> *In the beginning when God created the*
> *heavens and the earth, the earth was a*
> *formless void and darkness covered the face of*
> *the deep, while a* wind *from God swept over*
> *the face of the waters* (emphasis added).

Now look at how the New International Version translates the same text:

> *In the beginning God created the heavens and the earth. Now the earth was formless and empty, darkness was over the surface of the deep, and the Spirit of God was hovering over the waters* (emphasis added).

Was it a wind from God that hovered over the face of the waters, or the Spirit of God? Different translation committees make different calls.

THE HOLY SPIRIT IN THE OLD TESTAMENT

There are eighty to ninety references to the Spirit of God in the Old Testament, depending upon how one translates the Hebrew word *ruach*. In some cases the Spirit of God is said to be what gives each human being life. In several cases the Spirit is clearly the source of creative and artistic gifts, as was the case with the great artisan and craftsman Bezalel who lived in the days of Moses, as described in Exodus 31:2-5. Bezalel made beautiful things for God's tabernacle, and it was said that God's Spirit gave him such abilities.

Sometimes the Old Testament teaches that the Spirit is the source of superhuman strength, wisdom, and leadership. As early as Deuteronomy 34, we find leaders invoking or passing on the Spirit's leadership by laying hands upon their successors, a practice that would become commonplace in the New Testament: "Joshua son of Nun was full of the spirit of wisdom, because Moses had laid his hands on him" (Deuteronomy 34:9 NRSV). Later it was God's Spirit that "rested on," was "in," or "came over" the judges, great warriors, and leaders of ancient Israel.

One of my favorite pictures of the Spirit in the Old Testament comes in the stories about Samson, who had superhuman strength and was a great warrior delivering Israel from the hands of the Philistines. Over and over again, when Samson was faced with danger or confronted by overwhelming odds, the writer of Judges tells us (in the CEB), "The LORD's spirit rushed over him" or (in the NIV), "The Spirit of the LORD came powerfully upon him" (Judges 14:6, 19; and 15:14). Each time, the Spirit imbued Samson with amazing strength.

But while the Spirit often is described in the Old Testament as empowering and giving special gifts and abilities, the Spirit's most frequent work is in ensuring that God's voice is heard, so that God's purposes and will can be conveyed. For example, we see this work of the Spirit in 2 Samuel 23:2, where David declares, "The LORD's spirit speaks through me; his word is on my tongue."

One of the most famous references to the Spirit in the Old Testament is found in Isaiah 61:1, part of the text Jesus read during his first sermon in his hometown of Nazareth. In both Isaiah's day and Jesus' ministry, the Spirit's outpouring enables the proclamation of God's will: "The LORD God's spirit is upon me, because the LORD has anointed me. He has sent me to bring good news to the poor."

In Ezekiel 36:27 (NIV) God says, "I will put my Spirit in you and move you to follow my decrees and be careful to keep my laws." We see here the work of the Spirit in guiding God's people and influencing them to do his will.

In these examples, we can see that the Old Testament shows God's Spirit working primarily through the leaders—guiding, influencing, and speaking through them so that they pursue God's will.

In the New Testament, God's Spirit plays a different role, and we get a prophetic glimpse of that role in Joel 2:28, which looks ahead to the early church's expectation and experience of the Holy Spirit. There we read God saying, "I will pour out my spirit upon everyone; your sons and your daughters will prophesy, your old men will dream dreams, and your young men will see visions."

Among the key differences between the Old Testament and New Testament understandings of the Spirit is that most often in the Old Testament, the Spirit's work is for the remarkable and gifted leaders of Israel; whereas in the New Testament, Joel's words are fulfilled, and it is the unremarkable and the ordinary who receive God's Spirit.

THE HOLY SPIRIT IN THE NEW TESTAMENT

Compared with the eighty to ninety references to the Spirit in the Old Testament, the New Testament describes a veritable outbreak of the Spirit's work. It starts in the stories of both Jesus' and John the Baptist's conceptions in Luke's Gospel and explodes across the pages of the Acts of the Apostles, as the Spirit falls upon all believers. The New Testament contains too many mentions of the Spirit to recount them all here, so I'll limit my focus to John's Gospel and several compelling images of the Spirit.

Jesus calls the Spirit the *paraclete*. This Greek word comes from two words: *para*, which means close by, very near, or beside; and *kaleo*, from which we get our word *call*.

"Paraclete" is a term that was used in some legal circles to describe an advocate for the defense—a defense attorney—whose job was to come alongside or stand with the accused, serving as this person's advocate. Hence some versions of the New Testament translate *paraclete* as "advocate." Outside the judicial system, the word was also used to describe those who came alongside people who were hurting, to hold and comfort them. Hence *paraclete* is sometimes translated as "comforter" or "helper." In the Gospel of John, Jesus says the Spirit will guide us into truth, help us remember what Jesus taught, and flow like rivers of spring water within us.

We observed in Chapter 1 that God is a force that permeates everything and is the source of all that is: "In him we live and move and have our being" (Acts 17:28 NRSV). We described God as "being itself" and said that all creation is contingent upon him for its existence. In Chapter 2 we noted that Jesus showed us the being-ness of God, the essence of God who came to walk among us to reveal to us that God is and to show God's purposes, God's will, and God's character, as well as God's mercy, ultimately his triumph over evil, sin, and death. In this chapter, we find that the Holy Spirit is God's being—God's very presence—working *within* us, coming alongside us, and empowering, guiding, and shaping those who are open to his power.

Before his death, Jesus told his disciples that he would not leave them alone but would send the Spirit. The Spirit is God's *immanent* presence and power working in us. The Spirit does for us what the Spirit did for those of old: the Spirit empowers us. The Spirit imbues us with gifts and abilities to help others and to serve God. The Spirit leads and guides us. The Spirit uses us and speaks through us.

Just before Jesus left this earth, he told his disciples to wait in Jerusalem and he would send the Spirit: "You will receive power when the Holy Spirit has come upon you, and you will be my witnesses in Jerusalem, in all Judea and Samaria, and to the end of the earth" (Acts 1:8).

Note Luke's words in describing what happened on the Jewish feast of Pentecost shortly after Jesus' resurrection. As you read this passage, remember that the word for spirit also means "wind" or "breath."

> When the day of Pentecost had come, they
> were all together in one place. And suddenly
> from heaven there came a sound like the rush
> of a violent wind, and it filled the entire house
> where they were sitting. Divided tongues, as
> of fire, appeared among them, and a tongue
> rested on each of them. All of them were
> filled with the Holy Spirit and began to speak
> in other languages, as the Spirit gave them
> ability.
>
> (Acts 2:1-4 NRSV)

I love this imagery for the Spirit—a rushing, violent wind. But notice too the connection to the creation story in Genesis. There God breathed into and filled the man and woman, animating them and giving them life. Here God breathes upon Jesus' followers and fills them and makes them new. This is the re-creation of humanity by the work of the Holy Spirit.

THE VOICES WE LISTEN TO, THE POWERS THAT SHAPE US

Jack Levison, professor of Old Testament at Perkins School of Theology, described the biblical picture of the Holy Spirit in his book *Fresh Air*: "The spirit was a force to be reckoned with, an impulse to which mere humans capitulated, a source of daily breath and an uncontrollable outside power."[1]

The Spirit not only *was* a force to be reckoned with; to this day the Spirit *continues to be* that kind of force. I love this idea of the Spirit as a rushing mighty wind. The church I serve has been building its permanent sanctuary. One day while the building was under construction, I was standing in the midst of the sanctuary. The contractors had left for the day. The windows were not yet in and tarps hung across the openings. Suddenly a gale-force wind began to blow; some of the tarps came loose and were blowing and flapping in the wind making a tremendous amount of noise. I stood there, eyes closed, listening and praying that the Spirit would do in our sanctuary what the wind was doing that day: blowing with such force that worshipers would be moved, comforted, and filled with power.*

I think many Christians live Spirit-deficient lives, a bit like someone who is sleep-deprived, nutrient-deprived, or oxygen-deprived. Many Christians haven't been taught about the Spirit, nor encouraged to seek the Spirit's work in their

---

* If you ever visit Church of the Resurrection, look at the balcony railing around the room. It is subtly adorned with flames, a reminder of the Day of Pentecost and an invitation for the Spirit to descend upon worshipers with power as the Spirit descended upon the believers on the Day of Pentecost.

lives.* As a result, our spiritual lives are a bit anemic as we try living the Christian life by our own power and wisdom.

What are the voices you listen to, and what are the powers that shape your life? You've no doubt seen images of people who have a devil on one shoulder and an angel on the other, with each seeking to influence them. Personally, whether it's the devil or just my own shadow-self, I find there are voices in my own life that would lead me to give in to hate, indifference, desire, pride, infidelity, selfishness, or greed. But when we listen to the voice of the Spirit and open ourselves to the Spirit's active work in our lives, we find that we are led to a very different place and to become very different people.

The Spirit convicts us and quickens our conscience when we're doing wrong. The Spirit, through persistent nudges, urges us to act selflessly in our care for others. The Spirit makes us long to be more than we are at the present and to become more like the people God intended us to be. Paul describes the Spirit's work and its impact on our lives as the "fruit of the Spirit" in Galatians 5:22-23: "The fruit of the Spirit is love, joy, peace, patience, kindness, goodness, faithfulness, gentleness, and self-control." How different is this fruit than the fruit my own heart, and the culture around me, tends to produce in my life.

We'll return to the Holy Spirit's work in our lives in a moment. But for now, I'd like to consider the relationship

---

* I'm reminded of Paul's encounter with a group of disciples at Ephesus in Acts 19:1-2: "While Apollos was in Corinth, Paul took a route through the interior and came to Ephesus, where he found some disciples. He asked them, 'Did you receive the Holy Spirit when you came to believe?' They replied, 'We've not even heard that there is a Holy Spirit.'"

among the Father, the Son, and the Holy Spirit, a relationship Christians speak of as the doctrine of the Trinity.

THE HOLY SPIRIT AND THE DOCTRINE OF THE TRINITY

There is an interesting scene that occurs as Jesus begins his public ministry in the Gospels of Matthew, Mark, and Luke:

> *When Jesus was baptized, he immediately*
> *came up out of the water. Heaven was opened*
> *to him, and he saw the Spirit of God coming*
> *down like a dove and resting on him. A voice*
> *from heaven said, "This is my Son whom I*
> *dearly love; I find happiness in him."*
> *(Matthew 3:16-17)*

In this one scene we see the Father, the Son, and the Spirit. But Matthew doesn't tell us any more about the relationship among these three.

The three are mentioned in another scene, when near the end of Jesus' public ministry he speaks of returning to the Father. (Remember that he also has told his disciples in John 10:30 that "I and the Father are one" and in John 14:9 that "Whoever has seen me has seen the Father.") He then pledges in John 14:16 that after he returns to the Father, he will ask the Father to send the Spirit. Once again we find a tantalizing picture of Father, Son, and Spirit, but no explanation of their interrelationship.

Muslims and Jews understandably question whether Christians are truly monotheists, for to them it sounds as if we believe in three gods, not one. The New Testament authors never fully explain this to us. But the problem is not entirely a New Testament problem. Even in the Old Testament, as we've seen, there is mention of God and God's Spirit (*ruach*) as somehow distinct yet inseparable.

The Apostles' Creed mentions the Father, Son, and Spirit but provides no help in explaining the interrelationship among the three. It even adds to the confusion when it speaks of Jesus as "seated at the right hand of the Father." Is the Son really seated next to the Father? How are they one, yet sitting next to one another?

Christians believe in one God. We also believe the Father is God, the Son is God, and the Holy Spirit is God. How do we make sense of this? Christians spent more than four hundred years seeking to clarify what they believed and articulating it in the creeds, and yet fifteen hundred years later their answers can still be confusing.

While the idea of the Trinity is implicit in the New Testament, the word *Trinity* doesn't appear explicitly until the second and third centuries, in the writings of Tertullian, a Christian author, thinker, and theologian. The fact that the doctrine is not spelled out by the New Testament writers, nor unpacked by Jesus, should once again leave us with a great measure of humility in our statements about the Trinity, and an equally hefty measure of grace in hearing others speak about it. My own conviction is that the three pounds of gray matter we call a brain is not up to the task of fully comprehending the nature of God.

The work of theologians seeking to make sense of the Trinity might be compared to the work of physicists trying to explain how the world works at the subatomic level. In both cases, words have been created to explain something that the most intelligent of people struggle to comprehend. Explanations by the brightest theologians can sound, to ordinary people, like double-talk. I have a hunch that in heaven, even the brightest theologians will bow before God and say with wonder and awe, "So that's how it works!"

No one fully comprehends the Trinity. Our technical terms, analogies, and charts are our best efforts at explaining a paradox, a mystery, or a mind-blowing concept that our brains are ill equipped to handle.

I remember listening to a Christian radio program on which the host purported to have all the answers to any biblical or theological question the caller might have. Just once I wanted him to say, "You know, I just don't have a clue. Your question is above my pay grade!" On multiple occasions, I recall hearing him fielding questions about the Trinity. He would try to explain the doctrine, but if his explanation didn't seem to make sense to the caller, he'd say it again—only louder!

Be that as it may, both ordinary Christians and professional theologians rightly seek to explain the mystery of the Trinity. Professional theologians sometimes cringe when laity and pastors liken the Trinity to the three forms that H_2O can take—water, ice, and steam—preferring instead to use much "clearer" terms such as *homousias, substancia, persona*, and *perichoresis*! Yes, the analogies used by laity and pastors quickly break down, but so do technical Greek and Latin terms from the fourth and fifth centuries.

I'll share with you a couple of analogies that help me think about the Trinity, and one diagram that has been around since the 1200s as a way of visualizing the Trinity. As with any analogies, these all these break down fairly quickly, but I believe each illustrates some dimension of the Trinity as I understand it.

The Atom and the Trinity

The atom is a useful analogy for the Trinity. If you view any object at the highest magnification possible using an electron microscope, what you will see are atoms. Atoms are made up of three types of particles: protons, neutrons, and electrons.[*] An atom of, say, helium is not an atom of helium without protons, neutrons, and electrons. All three are essential to make an atom. The protons, neutrons, and electrons act upon one another and bind each to the others. Though we know today that atoms can be split, in ancient times the idea of an atom was that it was the smallest particle imaginable—thus the name, from the Greek *atemnein*, which meant "indivisible." Perhaps we could think of the atom, then, as analogous to God, the Indivisible One, who by his very nature is constituted of Father, Son, and Holy Spirit. These three are bound together such that God is not God without Father, Son, and Spirit, in much the same way that helium is only helium with a certain number of protons, neutrons, and electrons.

---

[*] The exception is hydrogen, which has only a single proton and a single electron with no neutrons.

Of course, when pushed there are a thousand ways the analogy breaks down, but taken at a simple level it may be helpful in illustrating the way that God is not God apart from Father, Son, and Holy Spirit.

The Human Being

We need look no further than ourselves to see another analogy, or perhaps a reflection, of the Trinity. What makes you "you"? It's not simply your body, nor your mind, nor your spirit; rather, all three of these things, taken together, make you who you are. A body is so important to you being you that, according to the Apostle Paul, when your earthly body dies you will be given a new body in heaven. Likewise, your mind is so important to your whole self that, in the event of a serious brain injury when someone is left in a persistent vegetative state, we ask if the individual is still there in any real sense. The person's body is present, but the mind, memories, and capacity to reason, to love, to live seems gone. Likewise, most human beings believe that we are more than a brain with a body, that we also have a soul or spirit that really defines who we are. All three of these components—body, mind, and spirit—are essential to being an individual human, at least as we walk on this earth. These components are interconnected and interrelated; one might even say that through them we experience something of God's Trinitarian nature in our own human existence.

Again, the analogy quickly breaks down, but for at least a moment it helps us begin to think about God as three-in-one.

Shield of the Trinity

In addition to analogies, sometimes seeing a visualization of an abstract concept can be helpful. I would offer a diagram that some have found helpful in identifying what Christians believe about God's triune nature. Beginning in the early 1200s, if not before, Christians used something called the Shield of the Trinity or *Scutum Fidei* (Latin for "shield of faith") to teach the orthodox understanding of this doctrine.

As you can see in the diagram, it is clear that the Father, Son, and Holy Spirit are distinct entities (the classic technical term was *personae*)—that is, the Father is not the Son, the Son is not the Spirit, the Spirit is not the Father. But the Father *is* God, the Son *is* God, and the Spirit *is* God. The diagram captures the idea of "God in three persons, blessed trinity."[2]

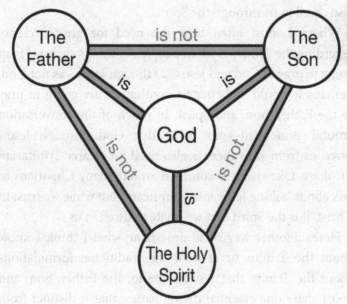

Further Thoughts About the Trinity

The idea of the Trinity includes several important concepts that are also quite practical. When we pray, regardless of whom we address in prayer, we are speaking to one God who is Father, Son, and Spirit. When we talk about God, we are referring to one God who is Father, Son, and Spirit. Though the Father is associated with the creation of all that is, and the Son with the redemption of the cosmos, and the Spirit with sustaining the cosmos, each "person" of the Trinity is involved, by virtue of their shared essential deity, in creating, redeeming, and sustaining. So God the Father doesn't merely send his Son to suffer and die for us; the Father and the Spirit share together in the Son's suffering for humanity. And the Spirit doesn't by itself fill God's people; the Father and the Son also dwell in us through the Spirit.

Where I most often hear the need for greater clarity regarding the Trinity is when people say things such as "I am going to pray to God and Jesus," as though Jesus was not God. Perhaps it would be better to say that we are going to pray to the Father, Son, and Spirit. In much of the conversation around atonement—our belief that God, through Jesus, saved us from sin—there is also need for clearer Trinitarian theology. Likewise it is common among many Christians to talk about "asking Jesus into your heart," but while we trust in Christ, it is the Spirit that we invite to dwell in us.

Here's another way of summarizing what I think I know about the Trinity, or at least the traditional formulations about the Trinity that I subscribe to: the Father, Son, and Spirit share one essential divine nature that is distinct from everything else in all creation. That divine nature, essence, or "stuff" of God is omnipresent—God permeates all creation and holds it together—and yet the divine essence is distinct from creation.

This one substance that is God is indivisibly Father, Son, and Spirit. Each member of the Trinity thinks, wills, and acts. The three are in an inseparable relationship with one another that reflects love, community, and a unity of being and purpose. They are one, and because there is one essence that is God, whatever one member of the Trinity does, the other members do as well, whether they are creating, redeeming, or sustaining. Wherever one member of the Trinity is (in "heaven," on the cross, in the human heart), the others are as well.

I'm aware that all this language fails us at many points, and that every analogy, diagram, and summary statement about the Trinity only takes us so far in understanding it. And despite the fact that I've attempted to explain what I think I know about the triune nature of God, it still makes my brain hurt to think about it. In the end, this is a paradox (perhaps *mystery* is a better word), much like many things seem to be in the realm of physics. I think I understand a bit, and I trust where my understanding fails. I continue to believe that when I die, I too will fall on my knees in awe and wonder and will finally comprehend what on this side of eternity seems nearly incomprehensible. What I do find comprehensible is that the Father is God, the Son is God, and the Spirit is God.

WELCOMING, LISTENING FOR, AND BEING SHAPED BY THE SPIRIT

Now that you fully understand the Trinity—you do fully understand it now, right?—OK, now that we've at least talked about the Trinity, let's turn to consider why our belief in and experience of the Holy Spirit matters.

You've no doubt experienced the Holy Spirit and may not have known it. Christians believe the Spirit is at work all around us all the time. I often feel a nudge—a thought that comes across my mind, to call on someone I hadn't thought of in a while or to speak with someone I might otherwise have walked by. I've learned to pay attention when I feel the nudge, as almost always something important happens when I follow it. At times I ignore this and miss out on something important.

The week I was writing this chapter, at about 11:50 P.M. I felt a nudge to go visit a woman who was dying of cancer in the hospital. I sent an e-mail to a member of her family but did not receive a reply. I didn't have a phone number to call any of the family. I decided rather than go to the hospital, I'd just pray for her and see her in the morning. When I woke up the next morning I learned that the woman had passed away just after midnight with her family surrounding her. I think I was supposed to be there, but I didn't take the nudge seriously.

Fortunately, there are many times when I do pay attention, act upon the nudge, and find myself in just the right place at just the right time to offer hope or comfort or care to someone in need.

There are times when some flash of insight comes to me that I'd never thought of before, and often I believe this is the Spirit's work. There are moments when I feel the presence of God in my life in the form of warmth, love, or a sense of peace.

Many times after worship I'll hear from church members who say, "I feel like your message was just for me today—it's exactly what I needed to hear." I believe this, too, is the Holy Spirit at work, taking my feeble attempt at a sermon and using it as a vehicle to speak to God's people.

Most of these experiences, I believe, are the work of the Holy Spirit.

I want to end this chapter by repeating the idea that the Holy Spirit is God's presence at work upon and within you. Long before people become Christians, the Holy Spirit is working to woo and beckon them to God. We speak of this work of the Spirit as God's prevenient grace. As I look back over my life I can see moments when God was at work long before I was a Christian, and in each case I would ascribe this work to the Holy Spirit.

When we finally decide to trust in Christ, it is the Spirit that works in us to reconcile us to God. We describe this work of making us right with God as God's justifying grace, and it too is a work of the Holy Spirit. After being brought into right relationship with God we're meant to be transformed, becoming the person God intends us to be. This process of transformation is referred to as sanctification. And this too is a work of the Holy Spirit, forming and shaping us from the inside out.

To recap, in our daily Christian life, it is the Spirit that nudges and beckons us this way or that. It is the Spirit that helps us pray. It is the Spirit that equips us with gifts to serve others. It is the Spirit that grants us the strength and grace to become increasingly like Christ. When we open ourselves to the work of the Holy Spirit, we find power to be transformed and to be useful in fulfilling God's purposes.

Pentecostalism and the Baptism of the Spirit

I came to faith in a small Pentecostal church. It was a wonderful congregation. Pentecostals are Christians who place a strong emphasis on the work of the Holy Spirit and who believe that the Spirit continues to work today in many of the same ways the Spirit worked in the early church as seen in the New Testament's Acts of the Apostles. There is an emphasis on experiencing the Holy Spirit and on the Spirit's ability to work supernaturally in one's life. Pentecostals anticipate and seek deeply moving experiences of the Spirit, the working of miracles, and the Spirit's providing words of insight or knowledge that are helpful for a particular individual or set of circumstances. Pentecostals place a strong emphasis on conversion, study of Scripture, and sharing of faith, as well as an infilling of the Holy Spirit subsequent to salvation, called the baptism in or of the Holy Spirit. Many Pentecostals believe that one's receiving the baptism of the Holy Spirit is evidenced by talking in an unknown language, or what they call "speaking in tongues."

The modern Pentecostal movement had its roots in Methodism, among other Christian movements. Charles Parham, one of the two early founders of modern

Pentecostalism, began his ministry as a Methodist circuit rider. William Seymour, one of the other formative leaders of the Pentecostal movement in America, came to faith in The Methodist Episcopal Church. Pentecostalism, from my vantage point, was a reaction to the failure of late nineteenth- and early twentieth-century Christianity to adequately emphasize the work of the Holy Spirit and the experiential side of the gospel. Early twentieth-century Christianity, particularly in the mainline churches, placed a strong emphasis on the intellectual side of the faith, and acts of piety and mercy, but had failed in helping people experience a faith that touched the heart.

Pentecostalism swept the country and the world like wildfire, with its emphasis on a personal relationship with Jesus Christ, the power of God's Spirit to work in the lives of believers, and a passionate, emotive faith. In mainline and Catholic churches, Pentecostalism gave birth to the Charismatic Renewal.

Today, Pentecostalism and the Charismatic Movement are themselves going through a transition. The rapid growth they had once seen in America is diminishing. Younger generations are pushing back on some of the historic emphases of the Pentecostal revival. There are many, like me, who were deeply touched by Pentecostalism but ultimately made our way to mainline denominations. But the Movements' impact upon Christianity in the twentieth century was profound, in that it reminded the entire church that the Holy Spirit was still active, and it challenged Christianity to rediscover the Spirit's power.

Receiving the Holy Spirit

The power of the Holy Spirit can be felt not only in individuals but in the church. The Apostle Paul wrote to the Corinthians, "Don't you know that you are God's temple and God's Spirit lives in you?" (1 Corinthians 3:16). The *you* here is plural—Paul is referring to the church, the gathering of believers. I've walked the streets of ancient Corinth, and there were temples to the pagan gods on every corner. Temples were physical reminders of the gods they represented, and places where the gods were thought to dwell among the people. Paul wanted the small Christian community in Corinth to know that they, as a group of believers, were themselves a temple. The Spirit of God lived within their community, as it lives in yours. In the next chapter we'll speak more about the church and how the Spirit works in and through her to animate, lead, and empower.

Recently I was putting together a file cabinet in the basement of my house. I grabbed my power drill and headed downstairs. When I got ready to assemble the cabinet, I picked up the drill, pressed the trigger, and heard it slowly grind to a halt. I had failed to plug the battery into the charger the last time I had used it. Unwilling to wait for the battery to recharge or to go back upstairs and to the garage to retrieve a screwdriver, I used the drill manually, turning the screw around and around by rotating the entire drill manually in my hand. It was a ridiculous way to screw something together, and it took five times longer than it should have. This is what churches look like when they seek to be the church without drawing upon the Spirit's power.

In that same Letter to the Corinthians, Paul altered his wording slightly, thus shifting the analogy from the church to the individual. He writes, "Don't you know that your body is a temple of the Holy Spirit who is in you?" (1 Corinthians 6:19). Here, *you* is singular; Paul is speaking now to individual Christians. He says that the Spirit dwells in every believer, and that each of us is a living, breathing bearer of God's presence and reality in the world. Paul goes on to unpack that concept by saying that because your body is a temple of the Holy Spirit, you must "honor God with your body" (1 Corinthians 6:20). This implies that what we do with our bodies affects the Spirit's work in us.

But how do we receive the Holy Spirit? The Spirit is already at work in your life, seeking to speak to, call, form, shape, and empower you. But the Spirit will not force himself upon you.* You can resist the Spirit, or welcome and invite the Spirit to work in you. In the church I serve, every time we baptize a child, youth, or adult, we anoint their heads with oil and lay our hands on them and invoke or pray for the Spirit to be at work in them. We do the same as we confirm individuals in the church, anointing them and praying for the outpouring of the Holy Spirit upon them. But the invitation for the Spirit to

---

* The use of a masculine pronoun to describe the Spirit is the subject of some debate today. *Ruach* in Hebrew is feminine and *pneuma* in Greek is neuter while *spiritus* in Latin is masculine. When Jesus refers to the Spirit as a *paraklete* the male pronoun is used. Many have used "it" and "itself" to seek to avoid the challenge, but this implies a lack of personhood. In the end God, as noted earlier, transcends our human gender categories, and many have suggested that the Spirit might well capture the feminine dimension of God just as Father and Son capture the masculine dimensions of God. I have used "himself" here as this has been the historic practice, but felt it important to convey that this may not be the best pronoun with reference to the Spirit.

work in us is not limited to baptism and confirmation. *Every* morning I invite the Holy Spirit to work in me. I do the same thing when I bathe each morning. I ask God for his power. I invite God to lead me by his Spirit. I pray that the Spirit will use me and speak through me. And then I try to listen carefully.

This listening carefully is important. My experience is that the Spirit usually whispers rather than shouts. My wife sometimes says to me, "Could you please put your phone down? I'm trying to talk to you but you are not listening." Does that ever happen to you—someone is talking to you but you're not really paying attention, or you are talking to someone but he or she is not really paying attention to you? I believe the Holy Spirit regularly experiences this with each of us. The Spirit whispers, but the noise and distractions in our lives drown out the Spirit's still, small voice. I want to invite you to welcome the Spirit's work, and to listen.

A couple of years ago a dear church member, Duane Clark, was moved to Hospice House, a hospice care center near the church. Duane had been like a grandfather to one of our other members, Jennifer Westlake, whose family had known Duane since before she was born. Jennifer was a kindergarten teacher who was also working on her master's degree at night. Jennifer's mother called her the day Duane moved into hospice, but by the time Jennifer finished class that night she was exhausted, so she decided to pray for Duane and then try to see him the next day.

In the middle of the night Jennifer was awakened. She told me, "I shot straight up in bed. There was a nudge and an overwhelming feeling that I was to go visit Duane at that very moment. It was the middle of the night, and I was tired, but the urge was relentless. So I got in my car and drove across town to Hospice House. I arrived, and Duane's sweet wife, Melba, was asleep. So I sat next to Duane and held his hand. I told him it was OK to go, that God was going to help make his transition peaceful and that our Father was waiting." Jennifer went on to say that just a few minutes later, Duane's breathing changed. Melba woke up, and in the middle of the night the two of them held Duane's hands as he took his final breath. Jennifer told me, "I am so thankful for the nudge of the Holy Spirit so that I could be there when Duane passed." This week, I failed to take seriously the nudging of the Spirit and was not there when a dear member of our church passed. Jennifer listened and paid attention and showed up at just the right time to usher Duane into Christ's arms.

At the beginning of this chapter I asked what voices you listen to. As we close the chapter I invite you to listen to the voice of the Holy Spirit, and to invite the Spirit to be at work in you, comforting, guiding, shaping, and empowering you. If you've never prayed to receive the Holy Spirit, you might take a moment to repeat this prayer.

Come Holy Spirit, I need you. Breath of God, fill me wholly and completely. Form and shape me into the person you want me to be. Lead me to do what you want me to do. Empower me and use me; speak to me and through me. Produce your fruit in me. Help me to listen to your voice above all other voices that clamor for my attention. Come, Holy Spirit, I need you. In Jesus' name. Amen.

4.

THE CHURCH AND
THE COMMUNION OF SAINTS

I believe in...
the holy catholic* church,
the communion of saints...

We learned in the last chapter that the community of believers, the church, is the temple of the Holy Spirit. Thus to explore our belief in the holy catholic church and the communion of saints is, in a very real sense, to unpack and clarify the work of the Holy Spirit.

Before thinking about what we mean by the church, I'd like to explore what is meant when the Creed affirms that the church that Christians believe in is "holy" and "catholic."

When many people view the church, it looks neither holy nor catholic. It seems filled with hypocrites and judgmental

---

* universal

people; in fact, this is one reason why many have turned away from "organized religion" and why so many young adults today say that they are "spiritual but not religious." Interestingly, these same young people have great admiration for Jesus but far less admiration for his people, the church. They see neither holiness nor catholicity when they look at the most vocal Christians and the most outspoken churches today.

It helps to understand that when we say we believe in the *holy* catholic church, we're not saying the church is filled with really righteous people who are nearly perfect. The word *holy* in the biblical context means belonging to God, or "sacred to" God or "set apart for" God. You've likely heard it said that the church is not a country club for perfect people, but instead a hospital for broken and sinful people who are slowly being made well.

The church, then, is holy when those who are a part of her recognize that she belongs to God and not to her members. She is holy when those who consider the church home don't ask "What do we want our church to do for us?" but rather "What does God want his church to do for him?" One metaphor for the church suggested by several passages in the New Testament is that of a bride, and specifically Christ's bride. Paul says a husband should love his wife as Christ loved the church and gave himself for her. Using this metaphor, the church is holy when she loves Christ and seeks to be faithful to him.

But what about the word *catholic*? As used here, *catholic* is an adjective. It does not refer to the Roman Catholic Church, at least not exclusively. *Catholic* comes from a compound Greek word that means, in essence, everywhere. (The Greek term *kata holos*, found in Acts 9:31, describes the church "throughout" Judea, the Galilee, and Samaria.) The word came to be a reminder of the church's unity: every community of believers across the Roman Empire and beyond was bound together in the gospel. Despite differences in language or ethnic makeup, these communities were a part of one church, the church everywhere, the catholic church.

Today, "Catholic" has come to mean a particular branch of the church dating back to the year 1054, when the Western church and Eastern church divided. In a remarkable bit of posturing, the Western church claimed the name Catholic—they were the "universal" church, or one might say the "real" church. The Eastern church claimed the name Orthodox, meaning "right worship" and by implication right beliefs and practices, hence they positioned themselves as the church who believed and worshiped in the "right" way. For Catholics, those who were not Catholic were not part of the universal church. For Orthodox, those who were not part of the Orthodox Church were . . . well, unorthodox, with wrong worship and wrong beliefs.

Tragically, today there are many divisions within the Christian family—more, it seems, every day. Jesus predicted this when he prayed in John 17 that God would make his followers one, as he and the Father are one. He tried to forestall the divisions among his followers by telling his disciples not to judge one another, and to love one another and forgive one another. Nevertheless, the church divided and continues to

Creed

divide. Despite this, our belief in the holy, catholic church is an ecumenical belief that all who call upon the name of Christ and seek to follow him as Savior and Lord are, despite their denominational or nondenominational names, part of one universal church. The Roman Catholic Church is a part of that one universal church, and so is the Eastern Orthodox Church, as well as the Lutherans, Presbyterians, Episcopalians, Baptists, Pentecostals, Methodists, nondenominational churches, and all the rest.

With this basic understanding of "holy" and "catholic," let's consider what Christians mean when they confess, as a central part of their faith, belief in the church.

WHAT IS MEANT BY THE WORD CHURCH?

Let's begin by defining the term: what does *church* mean? Most of us know already that the church is not a building, though we refer to buildings as churches. These buildings are actually the physical spaces that churches inhabit and use for activities such as worship, fellowship, Christian discipleship, and mission. Buildings are important tools, but the church is really *a people*.

The Greek word for "church" that is used more than eighty times in the New Testament is *ekklesia*, a word that literally means *called out*, as in a gathering of people called together. It was not a religious term but a secular term that often meant, simply, an assembly. It was used of synagogues, civic groups, and Christian gatherings. So, when you read "church" in the New Testament the word most often is the Greek word for assembly.

But church came to mean more than just an assembly when it referred to Christians. The first time we see this word in the Gospels is when Jesus speaks to Peter and says, "I tell you, you are Peter, and on this rock I will build my church, and the gates of Hades will not prevail against it" (Matthew 16:18 NRSV).

Here Jesus speaks of "my church," making it clear that the church is his ekklesia—his assembly. The church is specifically a community or assembly of people who belong to Christ. It is this relationship with Christ that distinguishes it from a synagogue, or a civic gathering, or a club. We see this same distinction in the other word used in the New Testament for church, which is the etymological source of our English word. The word is *kuriakon*, which means "belonging to the Lord." In German, *kuriakon* became *kirche*, which in English became church. The very name "church" means belonging to the Lord (as does the word *holy*, as we learned above). And when the word *ekklesia*—assembly—is translated as "church," it means specifically the assembly that belongs to Jesus. So in the New Testament, the church is the gathering of people called out by Jesus, who belong to Jesus, and therefore who seek not only to experience fellowship with him but to do his will and his work in the world.

Among the challenges many churches struggle with are issues of control. Who is in charge? Sometimes pastors act as though the church belongs to them. Some denominations act as though the church belongs to them. Some church leaders or staff or long-time members—the patriarchs and matriarchs of the church—believe or at least act like the church belongs to them. But the church is the Lord's. That means that the driving mission of every local church is to discern Christ's will above all else, and then to do it.

The church is made up of people whom the Lord claims as his own. I love how Peter says it: "Once you weren't a people, but now you are God's people" (1 Peter 2:10).

As human beings we need community. We need to belong. We need others to encourage us, challenge us, care for us, and be cared for by us. We are wired this way. As God is Father, Son, and Holy Spirit—each member of the Trinity in community with the others—we too are made for community. A wide array of studies have shown the importance of community in longevity and mental health. From a strictly secular perspective, we are healthier, happier, and live longer when we are in community with others. From a spiritual vantage point, we will never grow spiritually into the people God wishes us to be without the church.

Today there are many Christians who believe all the things I'm writing about in this book but who are not involved in a church. Maybe they've been hurt by a church in the past. It is inevitable that we'll be hurt from time to time by people in the church; I myself have experienced this on many occasions. But we don't give up on the church at those times, just as we don't divorce our spouses when they occasionally hurt our feelings.

Most people who leave the church slowly drift away. I've watched this happen hundreds of times. And so many essential things to the Christian spiritual life are lost when you don't have a community of others who are holding you accountable, helping you grow, needing you to serve, challenging you to care for others, praying with and for you, and giving structure to your Christian life.

The church is meant to be a unique community, unlike other clubs and organizations to which one might belong, though sharing some common characteristics with the best of these organizations. In what may have been his first letter, and the earliest document of the New Testament, Paul instructs the churches of the region of Galatia in what is today central Turkey, "Whenever we have an opportunity, let us work for the good of all, and especially for those of the family of faith" (Galatians 6:10 NRSV). Paul here uses another metaphor for the church—the church as a family. Nearly a hundred times in the New Testament, the apostles addressed the Christians they were writing to as "brothers and sisters." I love my siblings, but I don't get to spend as much time with them as I would like. There are people in the church with whom I will spend far more time and whom I love dearly, who, if I were in need of help at two in the morning, I would call without having to think twice. The idea of the church as a family comes with responsibilities: families care for one another, work for the good of one other, and support one another. In that same epistle, Paul instructed the members of these newly formed churches, "Carry each other's burdens and so you will fulfill the law of Christ" (Galatians 6:2).

The Greek New Testament word for this kind of caring for one another is *koinonia*, meaning "communion" or "sharing." We usually translate this word as "fellowship." It involves getting to know others, building relationships with them, and actively caring for and encouraging them. This was the purpose of the church—to foster, build, and serve as a community of people devoted to one another in brotherly and sisterly love, bound together by a common faith, and working together to live out their faith in the world. We not only are Christ's assembly; we are his family.

I have the joy of seeing this in action on a regular basis. Recently a good friend and staff member at the church I serve was diagnosed with cancer. Upon hearing the diagnosis, her friends began to pray, to listen, to love her. When she went in for surgery at seven in the morning, members of her small group were there, as well as other friends from the church who came to encourage and bless her. After her surgery, meals were brought over. People came by to offer love and care, and they all played a part in her recovery.

At our church, we talk about such people as "stretcher bearers," drawing the term from the story in the second chapter of Mark's Gospel, in which a man who had been paralyzed was carried on a stretcher by four of his friends to the house where Jesus was teaching. They could not get into the house because of the crowds, so these friends hoisted the man onto the rooftop, tore the roof off the house, and lowered him down in front of Jesus. What determination these friends showed in seeking their friend's healing! Mark tells us that Jesus was so moved by their faith and loyalty that he healed the paralyzed man. It was not the man's faith that led Jesus to heal the paralytic; it was the faith and determination of his friends.

This is what the church is meant to look like. The church is God's answer to our existential need for belonging, community, acceptance, support, and love. You don't ever have to be alone. If you are a member of a church, you are to take this seriously. It is part of your responsibility in being the church. It means looking around to see who is alone, who may need a friend, who needs encouragement. It means inviting people to sit by you, or asking if you can sit by them. It means checking on and caring for those who need someone. It means visiting the elderly and the sick. It means providing support and care for the hurting.

Not long ago, I was a part of a special baptismal service at one of our church's urban partners in Kansas City. The ministry is called Healing House, and it consists of a number of homes where persons just getting out of prison, or those who are looking to leave a life of addiction or prostitution, are welcomed and find the chance for a new life. Many of the residents are members of our church. The service took place on a Saturday morning, when a group of us gathered around an above-ground pool to witness fifty-one men and women being baptized or renewing their baptismal vows. It was deeply moving to see these persons immersed and then come out of the water feeling that, by God's grace, they were being made new. Almost as remarkable were the more than one hundred others who stood on the sidelines, cheering them on. With each baptism, people shouted and cheered and prayed. It was beautiful. What I saw that morning was the *ekklesia* of Jesus—the *kuriakon*—the church!*

---

* To find out more about Healing House, a nonprofit, faith-based recovery organization, check out their website at http://healinghousekc.org.

I know there are many dysfunctional congregations; in some way, every congregation likely has a bit of dysfunction. That's because churches are made up of imperfect people. We're going to get it wrong sometimes, preachers and lay people alike. And yes, the church is filled with hypocrites—we're all hypocrites, aren't we? No one perfectly lives the values and faith they espouse. But when the church is striving to be the church, she is one of the most beautiful communities in the world, a community that seeks to live selflessly, encourage and bless others, a community where you can be accepted as you are and where you will find family who will welcome you, stand by you, and encourage you.

You might be saying, "That's not what my church looks like." But here I'd ask, "What are *you* doing to help it be this kind of community?" Caring communities are made up of people who go the extra mile, who give up their time to serve others, who go out of their way to bless others. It only takes a handful of people like that to inspire others to do the same. Sometimes churches forget what it means to be the church. They don't need people who will stand by and criticize. They need people who will lovingly roll up their sleeves and model and live what it means to be the beloved community of Christ.

Occasionally I hear people say they don't need the church. I want to ask them: Really? You don't need encouragement from others, the blessings of worship and the Eucharist, a message drawn from Scripture, or a congregation that, like a family, stands together and has a greater impact on the world as a group than they could alone?

But even if they found some way to gain all these benefits without the church I would still say to them: if you are follower of Jesus, it's not just that *you* need the church, but that the *church* needs you! There are people at church who need you to show up, offer a word of encouragement, teach a class, lead a support group, or just stand at the door and welcome people. The church was not a human invention; it was founded by God. It's the temple of the Holy Spirit. It's a community that belongs to Jesus.

We live in a time when so many people are opting out of the church. Frequency of church attendance by Christians is down. Younger generations are dropping out. This may be in part because the church failed to be the church. But I think there's another reason. We've forgotten to teach what the church is and why it matters, and we've lost sight of the fact that the church isn't an optional add-on to your faith, but an essential part of being a Christian—something Jesus created to fulfill his mission. We are Christ's community.

We live in a time when millennials, the least churchgoing part of the population, are craving a community of deep friendships, bound together by common values, with an interest in positively affecting the world. That is precisely what Jesus intended the church to be.

THE CHURCH AS THE BODY OF CHRIST

The church is meant to be a community of redemption and love, a place of acceptance and transformation, a place where we grow in our faith and find encouragement and support—*koinonia.*

But the church isn't just about community. Listen to the words of Paul from 1 Corinthians 12:27: "You are the body of Christ and parts of each other." This image of the church as the body of Christ is really important. I take it to mean that the church incarnates Christ in the world today. God became flesh through Jesus, and in the same way Jesus, after his ascension to heaven, becomes flesh through the church. We are meant to continue the ministry that Jesus began, to re-present Jesus to the world. Jesus said it this way: "As the Father sent me, so I am sending you" (John 20:21). Immediately following this, "he breathed on them and said, 'Receive the Holy Spirit'" (John 20:22). Once more we find that the power and presence of the Holy Spirit are essential to the church in fulfilling Christ's mission in the world.

The idea bears repeating: The church is the continuing presence of Christ in the world. Jesus came two thousand years ago to show us the way, the truth, and the life, and to suffer, die, and rise again to save us; but before his departure he gave his disciples the Holy Spirit and called on them to be his ongoing presence in the world and to continue his saving work of healing, teaching, proclaiming, and liberating people.

So if we are the body of Christ, continuing the ministry of Jesus on this planet, we would do well to look to the Gospels to see the kinds of things Jesus did when he was walking on this earth, and then seek to do those things. Matthew summarized Jesus' earthly ministry in 9:35-38:

> *Jesus traveled among all the cities and villages,*
> *teaching in their synagogues, announcing the*
> *good news of the kingdom, and healing every*

> *disease and every sickness. Now when Jesus*
> *saw the crowds, he had compassion for them*
> *because they were troubled and helpless, like*
> *sheep without a shepherd. Then he said to*
> *his disciples, "The size of the harvest is bigger*
> *than you can imagine, but there are few*
> *workers. Therefore, plead with the Lord of the*
> *harvest to send out workers for his harvest."*

You will never prove intellectually there is a God, any more than others can prove there is no God. If you want to prove God's existence, show it by your actions. As part of the church, act as the body of Christ in the world; together we must incarnate God's love and Christ's presence. It is by our works of mercy, compassion, and service—not by Gospel tracts or theological debates—that we will draw people to Christ.

Roman Catholic theologian Cardinal Henri de Lubac expressed it well when he said, "If Christ is the sacrament of God, the Church is for us the sacrament of Christ; she represents him, in the full and ancient sense of the term, she really makes him present. She not only carries on his work, but *she is his very continuation*"[1] (emphasis added).

When God sees pain and brokenness, injustice and need in the world, he doesn't send angels to address it; he sends the church. There are 2.2 billion Christians in the world. Imagine the potential if everyone was a part of a community of the Lord's people, seeking to do his work in the world. And imagine how the world would be different if every church were seeking to continue Christ's work in the world around them.

Here's how Peter describes the church: "You are a chosen race, a royal priesthood, a holy nation, a people who are God's own possession. You have become this people so that you may speak of the wonderful acts of the one who called you out of darkness into his amazing light" (1 Peter 2:9).

I love this description! And how do we speak the wonderful acts of God? I think we do it most profoundly by our actions. It is by our love, compassion, kindness, and hunger for justice that we proclaim Jesus who called us out of darkness into his marvelous light. This is what it means to be the body of Christ. If you are not regularly asking, "Where does God need me?" and "How can I love and serve others?" then it is possible you are not yet a Christian. This is not to say that you can ever be saved by your good works, but that God's grace, freely given, was meant to lead you to good works.

The church I serve is a large congregation. Ten years ago I challenged our members: What if, when people think of our church, they don't first think of the size of our membership but instead of the size of our heart and the way that we serve the community? What if we were known not for our average weekly worship attendance but instead for the hours our members volunteer to address the needs of the city? And what if we were known not for how well we love each other but instead for how willing we are to welcome and love those outside the walls of our church?

Once again I turn to the words of Jesus to his disciples, the earliest expression of the church:

> *"You are the light of the world. A city on top of a hill can't be hidden.... Let your light*

shine before people, so they can see the good
things you do *and praise your Father who is
in heaven"*
 (*Matthew 5:14, 16* emphasis added*).*

At our best, the church is willing to take risks to love people
and push back the darkness of poverty, suffering, and injustice
while, through the good things we do, shining the light of
God's love, compassion, and mercy. In this way our actions
become a compelling testimony to the world of the truth and
power of the Christian gospel.

THE COMMUNION OF SAINTS

The Apostles' Creed goes on to speak of "the communion of
saints." When we think about this statement, it's important to
realize that the "saints" in the New Testament were not those
who had been canonized by the church after death; rather,
this was Paul's preferred way of referring to all Christians. He
addresses many of his letters either "to the saints" or "to those
who are called to be saints."

In this context, the Greek word for "saints" is *hagios*. The
word, or one of its variants, appears in the New Testament
235 times. As an adjective it is often translated as "holy." It
is used when the Bible speaks of the Holy Spirit. It is used to
describe God, or angels, or places and things that belong to
God or are set apart for God. It is used to differentiate something that is sacred from things that are mundane, profane,
ordinary.

For Christians, the word *saint* or *holy* refers to both a present reality and a future calling. As we learned earlier, the word has the sense of "belonging to God." Those who have yielded their lives to God, who seek to be God's people, who have accepted the redemptive work of Jesus, who have the Holy Spirit dwelling in them, are in a sense already holy. But in another sense they are not yet holy, in that holiness is also a calling and a goal to which they devote their lives—a call to be completely surrendered to God and to become the people God intends them to be.

Human beings share an inherent longing for meaning and purpose in their lives. Rick Warren tapped into this several years ago in his best-selling book *The Purpose Driven Life*. The call to be saints is, at its core, a call to the purpose for which God created us.

The calling to be saints and the process of becoming saints are what is meant by the term *sanctification*, from the Latin *sanctus*, which is roughly the equivalent of the Greek *hagios*. All Christians are called to belong wholly to Christ, to become like him. It is the call to love God with all that is within us. It is the call to love our neighbor as we love ourselves. This is not something we can simply try harder to do, though we should desire it and pour ourselves into the task. But ultimately the process of being transformed—of being "saint-ified" or sanctified—is only possible, Christians believe, by the work of the Holy Spirit. This is what Paul speaks of in 2 Corinthians 3:18:

> *All of us are looking with unveiled faces at*
> *the glory of the Lord as if we were looking in*

*a mirror. We are being transformed into that
same image from one degree of glory to the
next degree of glory. This comes from the Lord,
who is the Spirit.*

If we look at those we call saints throughout the history of the church, most were ordinary people who yielded their lives to God and through whom God worked in remarkable ways; people whose lives came to be defined by the way that they loved. I know so many "ordinary saints"—people who daily seek to love their neighbors, who "speak up for those who cannot speak up for themselves" (Proverbs 31:8 NIV), who show kindness and compassion for those who are hurting, who sacrifice themselves for others in ways that will never be publicly celebrated.

Ordinary saints take thirty minutes off work to donate blood and help to save the life of another. They turn off the lights when they leave a room in order to be good stewards of the earth's resources. They visit prisoners at the local state prison or show up for Friday night Bible study with formerly homeless people. They visit the elderly who have no family in town and work to do home repairs for them. They find ways to bless others without seeking recognition. They have a heart of compassion. These ordinary saints pay attention each day, watching for moments when God needs them to reach out to someone who needs care. They think less and less of themselves and more and more of others as they grow older. They seek to avoid evil and to do all the good that they can. They practice the things that help them grow in love for God and others.

I'm not the ordinary saint I want to be, but I'm on the journey, aided by the Holy Spirit and the church. Christians believe that when we pass from this life to the next, the Holy Spirit finally and completely sanctifies us, so that in heaven we are finally and fully the saints God intended us to be. When we see our loved ones in heaven, we will see them as God intended them to be, perfected in love.

There's one last thing to note about the phrase "communion of saints." It involves the word *communion* and is one of the most beautiful ideas in Christian theology. The idea is that those who are becoming saints here on earth, and those who have become entirely sanctified in heaven, still commune together.

From the time my daughters were born, I have prayed for them at least three times a day, and often five times a day. I've told them that when I die, I can't imagine that I would stop praying for them from heaven. I don't believe our loved ones who have died spend all their time watching over us from heaven—I don't really want them watching me all the time, seeing me at my worst, nor, as much as I love them, do I want to spend all my time in heaven watching my children and grandchildren! But I do think our loved ones who have died continue to love and care for us and await the day when we will be reunited. I think they do pray for us. While Protestants don't pray to saints, we can pray *for* them, and I believe we can ask God to share with them what is on our hearts. Every Mother's Day, I thank God for my grandmother Sarah, who played a pivotal role in my knowing God, and I ask him to tell her that I still remember her and love her. At other times I speak to God about friends who have died and are in God's presence, thanking God for them or praying that God would bless them and allow them to know they are missed.

I recently officiated at the wedding of a young woman whose father had died of cancer not long before. I shared with her that I believe the communion of saints means that there are moments in our lives here on earth when God says to those dear to us in heaven, "I want you to see something," and allows them to join us from above. I can't prove it by quoting a chapter and verse in the Bible, but when I think of the communion of saints, this is one example of what I think that looks like. As she married, a candle was lit on the altar in memory of her father as a way of recognizing that her father was still a part of her life as they were both a part of the communion of the saints.

When Christians gather for worship, we enter one of those "thin spaces" where heaven and earth meet. I believe we're never closer to our loved ones who have died and are with God in heaven than when we worship. I think this is what Charles Wesley was thinking of when he penned his well-known poem that later became the beloved hymn, "O For a Thousand Tongues to Sing."

> Glory to God, and praise and love
> be ever, ever given,
> by saints below and saints above,
> the church in earth and heaven.[2]

My office at the Church of the Resurrection is just outside one of our memorial gardens. This garden includes a waterfall, beautiful landscaping, and multiple columbaria—niches where those who are cremated may have their ashes interred. On many Saturdays when I step out of my office and head to the sanctuary to lead our Saturday evening worship service, I see a husband and wife from our church standing in the garden, next to the niche where their son's ashes are interred. He was a young man who died in a car accident. Sometimes I walk by and pray silently for them. Sometimes I step outside to greet them. They stop in the garden before going in to worship, pausing to pray for their son and remember him. As they join in worship, I believe they are closely connected with the saints above, bound together with them by the presence and love of God.

In Chapter 11 of the New Testament Letter to the Hebrews, the author describes the heroes and heroines of faith that came before his time, mentioning, among others, the patriarchs and matriarchs of ancient Israel. He begins the next chapter by writing,

> *Therefore, since we are surrounded by so great*
> *a cloud of witnesses, let us also lay aside every*
> *weight and the sin that clings so closely, and*
> *let us run with perseverance the race that is*
> *set before us, looking to Jesus the pioneer and*
> *perfecter of our faith.*
> *(Hebrews 12:1-2 NRSV)*

I love this image of a race, with the saints in heaven cheering us on as we run.

When Jesus came, he did not simply call individual disciples; he formed a community, a family, a people chosen to love and to continue his work in the world. This assembly or gathering is meant to be a foretaste of heaven, a place where people care for one another, encourage one another, and build one another up. But it is also meant to be a community, empowered and led by the Holy Spirit, that serves as the continuing presence of Christ in the world.

The church is holy because she belongs to God and is set apart for God's work. She is catholic because in God's eyes there is only one church, though it is made up of many tribes, nations, and denominations. God's church is a communion of "saints below and saints above" who are bound together as members of God's family.

I believe in the holy, catholic church and the communion of saints!

5.

THE FORGIVENESS OF SINS

I believe in...
the forgiveness of sins.

A friend, who was a bit skeptical of the Christian faith, once said to me, "Why is it that Christians are so obsessed with convincing people they are sinners and laying a guilt trip on them? Every time I go to church it feels like another guilt trip. What a depressing religion!"

It is certainly true that there are churches whose primary focus is on sin and whose weekly worship services are laden with guilt. And it's also true that some of the loudest and most vocal Christian voices in our country seem preoccupied with pointing out the sins of others. But that doesn't reflect the emphasis of the Christian faith as found in the Apostles' Creed. Notice that the Creed doesn't say, "I believe that human beings are sinners," though that is assumed. It says, "I believe in...the forgiveness of sins." The emphasis in both the Creed and the Christian faith is not on guilt, but grace; it is not on sin, but forgiveness.

Of course, Christianity's affirmation of the forgiveness of sins doesn't mean much if we don't understand that we need forgiveness. Forgiveness is an answer to a problem, a spiritual cure for a spiritual illness. And if you don't understand that you have a problem, you won't avail yourself of its solution.

As Donald Trump was campaigning for the Republican nomination for president in 2016 he was asked, "Have you ever asked God for forgiveness?" He replied, "I'm not sure I have. I just go and try and do a better job from there....If I do something wrong, I think I just try to make it right. I don't bring God into that picture. I don't."[1] He created quite a stir among many religious people, so he tempered the comments a few days later. But I think he was being honest, and his comments reflect the way many people feel: in theory they believe in the forgiveness of sins, but the concept doesn't really apply to them.

Standing in stark contrast to this view is one articulated by twentieth-century existentialist theologian Paul Tillich, who once said, "Forgiveness is an answer, the divine answer, to the question implied in our existence."[2]

What are the questions implied in our existence to which forgiveness is God's answer? I'll divide this chapter into three broad questions that will help us see what Tillich may have had in mind: Who needs forgiveness? Will God forgive *my* sins? Must I forgive others?

WHO NEEDS FORGIVENESS?

Belief in the forgiveness of sins is only good news if we first understand that we need forgiveness, and to make sense of that understanding we must talk about sin. Here I'd remind you of what was mentioned earlier in the book—that the primary word for sin in the New Testament is *hamartia*, a term used by archers that meant "to miss the mark." This was a great word to use in illustrating what sin is, particularly in a day when people hunted with bows and arrows. Just as an archer's arrow might miss the intended target, we as human beings miss the target in our thoughts, words, and deeds. The word points to a fundamental existential truth: there is an ideal we're meant to live up to as human beings—in the last chapter we called it holiness, or sanctification—but we all fall short of this ideal, mark, or target. The theological word for missing the mark is sin, and because we daily miss the mark— saying, thinking, or doing things we should not have done, or failing to say, think, or do things we should have done—we find ourselves in need of forgiveness.

What does "missing the mark" look like? The fourth-century desert father Evagrius Ponticus is credited with outlining a list of foundational or cardinal sins from which all other sins arise. The list became known in Christianity as the "seven deadly sins." I find the list helpful in examining my own life to see where I miss the mark. There are variations in the lists of these deadly sins, depending upon how certain Latin words are understood and translated, but here is one standard list:

- lust
- gluttony
- greed
- sloth
- anger
- envy
- pride

Most of these seven deadly sins are pretty self-explanatory, though a word about sloth might be helpful. I understand sloth to be not only avoidance of doing what we're meant to do, but indifference to evil or the suffering of others. Going back to the list, which of us hasn't struggled with these sins? Some are a daily struggle for me.

Another way to look at "missing the mark" is to think of the virtues our lives are meant to be defined by. There are a variety of lists describing such virtues. As noted earlier, one such list is Paul's "fruit of the Spirit," in which he paints a picture of the marks by which God intends to define our lives, including "love, joy, peace, patience, kindness, goodness, faithfulness, gentleness, and self-control" (Galatians 5:22-23). With the Spirit's help, we hope to achieve these virtues, but looking over the list, it is easy for most of us to see that we miss the mark.

A traditional prayer of confession used in Anglican and Methodist settings captures the variety of ways we sin and helps us understand our need for forgiveness:

Most merciful God,
we confess that we have sinned against you

in thought, word, and deed,
by what we have done,
and by what we have left undone.
We have not loved you with our whole heart;
we have not loved our neighbors as ourselves.
We are truly sorry and we humbly repent.[3]

To be clear, we sin by things we've thought, said, and done (sins of commission), but we can also sin by failing to think, say, or do things we should have done (sins of omission). Either way, sin is a failure to be or do what God intends for us as human beings. It is a missing of the mark.

Sin can enslave us. It can rob us of joy. The lure of sin over-promises and under-delivers. I've seen up close the impact of surrendering to lust, gluttony, greed, sloth, anger, envy, and pride. We see the impact of sin every day on the evening news. In the last century, hundreds of millions of people died needlessly due to war, greed, ethnic violence, terrorism, unclean water, lack of food and health care, and more—and the underlying causes of all of these things can be summarized by one word: *sin.*

It's easy to look at the categories of sin I've just mentioned and think they apply to the sins of others, while not seeing our own struggle with sin. That's where Alexandr Solzhenitsyn's words offer an important truth:

If only there were evil people somewhere insidiously committing evil deeds, and it were necessary only to separate them from the rest of us and destroy them. But the line dividing good and evil cuts through the heart of every human being.[4]

The Apostle Paul offers this realistic assessment of the human condition when he writes, "All have sinned and fall short of God's glory" (Romans 3:23). We've all treated others poorly, been self-absorbed, and failed to do justice and practice loving-kindness. We're all difficult to live with at times. We've all missed the mark.

In the New Testament there are several senses in which the word *sin* is used. One sense, as we've noted, is missing the mark—thinking, saying, and doing things that are unloving; and *not* thinking, saying, and doing things we should have done if we were loving. But there is another sense in which the word *sin* is used in the New Testament. Paul speaks of sin as a force, drive, or power that is at work in us, something that is broken or marred in us that lures us, or seeks to compel us to do the things we should not do, and to fail in doing the things we should. As Solzhenitsyn noted, this is the line dividing good and evil that cuts through every human heart.

We pretend that sin has no power over us and that we're not really sinners, but maintaining this illusion shows a lack of self-awareness—and self-awareness is the very thing we need in order to turn away from sin and resist its power. So long as I don't see my own inner tendency to be self-absorbed, materialistic, lustful, boastful, unloving, stingy, and more, I'll find it easier not only to surrender to those tendencies but to justify them as well. If, by contrast, I'm aware of my own sin and the impulses at work in me, I'm better able to struggle against sin and seek to overcome it.

Among the many effects of sin in our lives is an alienation or separation not only from God but from others. A man I knew years ago would routinely say things that were hurtful to others without being self-aware enough to see it. When people tried to point this out to him, he justified his behavior and dismissed them. Over a period of years he alienated every friend and person who sought to be a friend, until by the end of his life he had no one left.

At any point along the way, this man could have been reconciled with many of his friends if he'd only been self-aware enough to see and admit his sin, and ask his friends for their forgiveness.

Who needs forgiveness? Human beings need forgiveness. All of us do.

WILL GOD FORGIVE MY SINS?

Some people don't think they need to be forgiven and can't see the sin in their own lives; but on the opposite end of the spectrum, I have known other people who are uncertain God can or will forgive them. Some of these people carry guilt or shame with them from events long past; others take up a new load of guilt every day. My Roman Catholic friends describe this as "Catholic guilt," an overly active conscience that leaves one in a perpetual state of guilt; but it's not unique to Catholics.

At times the awareness of our sin is like being shackled by a heavy burden. I think of a man who decades earlier had, in fear, run away instead of stopping to help a friend who had been attacked. The friend later died from injuries sustained in the attack. The man came to my office saying that he could never forgive himself for running. For nearly forty years he had carried this burden, reliving it over and over again. He struggled to believe that God would ever forgive him, let alone that God already had.

That example is extreme. Most of us have known feelings of guilt over far less dramatic events. Feeling some measure of guilt is not necessarily a bad thing. We're meant to feel remorse when we've done something wrong. These feelings move us to repentance, to reconciliation, and to avoiding the same behavior in the future.

But some people struggle with excessive guilt, and it's often because their conception of God is inadequate. They feel displeasure from God where there is no displeasure. They feel guilty when they are enjoying life, as though God doesn't wish them to have joy. They feel they can never do enough to measure up to God's expectations, and yet one of the fundamental assertions of the Scriptures is that God is rich in mercy and abounding in steadfast love.*

I'm reminded of J. B. Phillips's classic little book *Your God Is Too Small*. Phillips notes that many of us have conceptions of God shaped by our parents or by other Christians that do not reflect the heart and character of God. Among the misconceptions that Phillips mentions is the God of "absolute perfection" who requires that his children be perfect. Phillips notes that this conception of God "has taken the joy and

---

* The concept that God is "rich in mercy and abounding in steadfast love," is found throughout the Old Testament. Examples include Exodus 34:6; Numbers 14:18; Psalms 103:8; 145:8; and Joel 2:13. The fact that the text appears scattered throughout the Old Testament is surprising to some, who imagine that the Old Testament God is vengeful; but the dominant picture of God in the Old Testament is more often one of mercy.

spontaneity out of the Christian lives of many...who dimly realize that what was meant to be a life of 'perfect freedom' has become an anxious slavery."[5]

As we learned in Chapter 2, Jesus came to reveal God's character and will, and from his birth to his resurrection, Jesus offered grace for sinners. We also learned that when the angel appeared in a dream to Joseph, announcing that Mary would bear a son, Joseph was instructed, "You will call him Jesus, because he will save his people from their sins" (Matthew 1:21).

Throughout the Gospels Jesus told parables about God's willingness to forgive sins. Jesus was known by his critics as a "friend of sinners." Large crowds of people who felt alienated from God came to hear him. He was constantly offering forgiveness to people who clearly needed to know that their lives could be made new.

On the night before his crucifixion, at the Last Supper, Jesus took bread and wine and said, "Take and eat. This is my body....Drink from this, all of you. This is my blood of the covenant, which is poured out for many so that their sins may be forgiven" (Matthew 26:26-28). As he hung on the cross, he looked at his persecutors and prayed, "Father, forgive them, for they don't know what they're doing" (Luke 23:34). Jesus turned to the thief on the cross and said, "Today you will be with me in paradise" (Luke 23:43). After his resurrection, Jesus told his disciples, "The forgiveness of sins must be preached in his name to all nations" (Luke 24:47). Jesus revealed a God who is more willing to forgive than we are even to ask.

As a pastor I've heard many confessions over the years. I've listened as people told me they betrayed trusts, violated the law, and failed as parents. I've heard people confess their affairs and disclose their addictions. Then, together, we talk about what true repentance looks like and what it would mean to make amends. We talk about why what they did was wrong, how it affected others, how God may have experienced their sin, and what they have learned from their experience. And then we talk about grace and the character of God as revealed in Jesus. We talk about atonement and forgiveness. Then I invite them to imagine Christ bearing the weight and burden of their sin on the cross.

Once when I was preaching on grace to our congregation, I had with me a thirty-five-foot-long chain of half-inch links. The chain weighed fifty pounds. I spoke about the sins we've all committed in thought, word, and deed—what we've done and what we've left undone—and I likened these sins to the links in the chain. As I listed many of the common sins we all struggle with, I wrapped the fifty-pound chain around my neck, crisscrossing it over my shoulders and back around my neck again. By the time I finished listing sins, I struggled to breathe, and my shoulders were slumped. The congregation could feel the weight of these chains.

I reminded the congregation that when Jesus taught his disciples to pray for God to forgive their trespasses (Matthew 6:12), the Greek word in the text for "forgive" was *aphiemi*, a word that means "to release." We are asking Christ to release us from this burden of guilt. We can choose to carry the burden of our sin and guilt, or we can choose to accept God's forgiveness and to allow him to release us from this burden. When we trust in Jesus' words about God's mercy, and believe that God has released us from our sins, we also must release this burden.

We can ask for God's forgiveness, yet choose to continue to hold on to our guilt. Or we can trust, with the Apostle Paul that "Christ Jesus came into the world to save sinners" (1 Timothy 1:15). And with the psalmist we can recognize that

> *God won't always play the judge;*
> *he won't be angry forever.*
> *He doesn't deal with us according to our sin*
> *or repay us according to our wrongdoing,*
> *because as high as heaven is above the earth,*
> *that's how large God's faithful love is for*
> *those who honor him.*
> *As far as east is from west—*
> *that's how far God has removed our sin*
> *from us.*
>
> *(Psalm 103:9-12)*

When we say in the Creed, "I believe in…the forgiveness of sins," we are affirming the truth of Scripture that God is willing to forgive us and wants to release us from our burdens. God's desire is that we repent and turn away from the sins we've committed and the burdens of sin and guilt that weigh us down.

It is believed the Apostles' Creed was first written to be recited when individuals were converting to the Christian faith, just before baptism. The converts were affirming their faith in God—Father, Son, and Holy Spirit—and in the church, and in the fact that God forgives sins, and in the truth that Jesus bore the burden of our sin on the cross. Stepping into the water, those being baptized knew that their past sins were being forgiven, and that God was promising, in advance, to forgive their future sins.

I mentioned in the previous chapter the joy of participating in a baptismal service for fifty-one men and women of Healing House who had chosen to become Christians. Many were former addicts. Some were previously prostitutes. One of the women was baptized with her daughter. She told me that her drug addiction led her to lose her home, sleep in her car, and be imprisoned on several occasions. As a result, she had "lost what was most precious to me, my two beautiful children." At Healing House she found new life. She has her children back. She is living sober. She said, "Being baptized gave me the chance to wash away my sins and to be forgiven by my heavenly Father.... The best part is, now I get to teach my kids and lead by example how to be a faithful follower of Jesus." As she and the others were baptized, all of us were experiencing what we affirm in the Creed: we believe in the forgiveness of sins.

You don't have to be defined by the worst things you've ever done. And you don't have to be tomorrow who you were yesterday. God *wants* to forgive you. God is the God of the Second Chance. Jesus suffered and died to redeem you. Ours is a gospel of redemption. God offers new life for old, grace and redemption for guilt and shame. And we can, and likely must, claim this every day.

MUST I FORGIVE OTHERS?

When we say that we believe in the forgiveness of sins, we're not only confessing that we are sinners, nor only that God is willing to forgive us; we also are expressing what is taught throughout Scripture, that *we* are called to forgive the sins of others.

Jesus teaches this over and over again in the Gospels. In the Lord's Prayer we say, "Forgive us our trespasses, *as we forgive those who trespass against us.*" I wonder how many people stop to think about this phrase when they say the Lord's Prayer. When we pray it we are asking God to forgive us *in the same way, and to the same degree,* that we extend forgiveness to others. In the Gospel of Matthew, after teaching the prayer, Jesus goes on to make this point crystal clear: "If you forgive others their sins, your heavenly Father will also forgive you. But if you don't forgive others, neither will your Father forgive your sins" (Matthew 6:14-15). What an unnerving statement!*

Going back to our chain metaphor, if we don't forgive others when they seek our forgiveness, we're refusing to release them from the heavy chains of guilt and shame they may be carrying. But in another sense, our unwillingness to forgive—and by this I mean to relinquish or release the right of retribution—means taking a new set of chains upon ourselves, chains of bitterness and resentment.

I've known so many people over the years who were unwilling to let go of the bitterness and resentment they felt

---

* A similar statement is made by Jesus in Matthew 18:21-35 when Peter asks how often he should forgive.

toward another. They would meditate upon the wrong done to them, mulling it over again and again. The disappointment or resentment would lead to anger and hate. You've likely heard some version of this quotation: "Holding on to resentment is like drinking poison and hoping the other person gets sick."*

Remember, forgiving others is not the same as saying that what the individual did was OK; rather, it's choosing not to hold on to the wrong done to us, nor to hold it over the head of the one who wronged us.

Forgiveness also doesn't necessarily release the one who sinned from all consequences. Sometimes consequences are themselves redemptive. Consequences may be legally required, and the failure to have consequences may keep the one who has sinned from changing.

Likewise forgiving is not the same as forgetting, at least not for us as humans. Years ago a friend violated a confidence and shared something I'd told him to keep to himself. He later apologized, and I gladly accepted his apology, but after that I was much more cautious in what I shared with him.

There's a lot more to the subject of forgiveness—asking for forgiveness, accepting God's forgiveness, forgiving ourselves, forgiving others. I've written an entire book on the subject.** But as we consider what Christians believe and why, it is a witness to the centrality of forgiveness to the Christian gospel that, despite the brevity of the Apostles' Creed, the statement "I believe in... the forgiveness of sins" made the cut.

---

* The quotation is often attributed to Nelson Mandela, but it goes back before his time, though no one is quite sure who first said it.

** Adam Hamilton, *Forgiveness* (Nashville: Abingdon Press, 2012).

A woman in the congregation I serve wrote me some time ago about forgiveness and its power. The woman said she had been struggling with an autoimmune disease that had left her disabled, and she had come to believe that her unwillingness to forgive others was actually contributing to the illness. She noted that in an autoimmune illness, the body attacks itself, in much the same way that she felt her bitterness and resentment were attacking her mind and spirit. The woman told me that when she finally made the decision to forgive, to release others of their emotional debts, and to relinquish her right to retribution or resentment, it was as if she experienced an immediate remission (literally, gaining a new mission in life). Forgiveness brought about a healing of her heart that resulted in relief from much of her physical pain. The woman wrote, "For me, forgiveness may just be the most powerful medicine there is."

Another woman wrote to tell me that her cousin had disappeared more than two decades ago. At the time, many people had believed her cousin's boyfriend had killed her, but nothing was ever proved. She told me that for years she had dreamed of slowly strangling the boyfriend and killing him. She wrote, "I know how it feels to have the hate and anger and sadness eat you up inside. When you carry that much negative [emotion] you eventually have to decide to hold on to it forever and let it become who you are, or you release it and refuse to carry it anymore. [One day] I chose to let it go." When the woman forgave the boyfriend, releasing him from her hate and her right to get even, she finally found freedom.

Creed

You've heard it before: you can get bitter or better. Again, forgiving others is not saying that what happened didn't matter. It is saying, "I choose to release you, and I choose to release me."

Forgiveness is a central part of Christian faith. As Paul Tillich noted, it is "the divine answer, to the question implied in our existence."[6] When we confess that we believe in the forgiveness of sins, we are recognizing that all of us need forgiveness; we are affirming that God is willing to forgive our sins; and we are accepting Christ's call to forgive others.

I believe in the forgiveness of sins!

6.

THE RESURRECTION
OF THE BODY

I believe in …
the resurrection of the body
and the life everlasting. Amen.

Before delving into the final lines of the Creed, which focus on the afterlife, I'd like to mention briefly something that may already be apparent to you. The Apostles' Creed offers a very short list of things that were considered essential to confess if one were to be baptized as a Christian. (Remember, this seems to have been the purpose of the Creed in its initial formulation.) As a result, many of the things that various Christians believe today, and are willing to fight over, are not found in the Apostles' Creed, nor in any of the other Creeds that date from the first five centuries of Christianity.

Concerning these additional opinions and beliefs, which are neither clearly articulated by the early church in the Scriptures nor found in the creeds, it might be well to hold the view of Peter Meiderlin, a Lutheran theologian who in the early 1600s said something like this: "In essentials, unity; in nonessentials, liberty; and in all things, charity."*

The Creed ends where Easter begins, with the resurrection and the promise of life everlasting. Lent begins on Ash Wednesday, when Christians confess their sin and recall their own mortality; as the ashes are placed on the forehead the one placing the ashes there will often say, "Remember that you are dust, and to dust you shall return" and/or "repent and believe the good news"—each statement pointing to the dual emphasis on sin and death. The season reaches its climax on Good Friday, when Christ died for our sins, and on Easter morning, when he rose victorious over death. Jesus' death and resurrection are the antidotes to human sin and mortality. In this final chapter, we'll consider the promised return of Christ, the Last Judgment mentioned earlier in the Creed, the resurrection of the body, and the life everlasting.

WHAT HAPPENS TO US WHEN WE DIE?

It's a question that all human beings ask at different times in their lives: what happens to us when we die? The question

---

* This quotation is often wrongly attributed to either John Wesley or St. Augustine, but it was Meiderlin who said these words: "If we might keep in necessary things unity, in unnecessary things freedom and in both charity, our affairs would certainly be in the best condition." Some, however, have suggested that a Catholic archbishop named Marco Antonio de Dominis wrote something similar a few years before Meiderlin. See: https://douglasbeaumont.com/2013/06/18/the-origin-of-in-essentials-unity/.

doesn't simply ask what happens to our bodies; it asks, more importantly, whether any part of us continues to live after our bodies have died. Is there something more? Is there an afterlife? To all these questions the Creed answers a definitive *yes!*

As far back as we can tell, human beings appear to have wondered about this question and to have hoped that we survive death. The earliest undisputed intentional human burials date back eighty thousand to one hundred thousand years. Interestingly, these ancient burials were found in the Holy Land, in locations called Qafzeh, near Nazareth, and Skhul Cave, on the side of Mount Carmel. Both sites show intentional burials, including pigments used to mark the dead, as well as rudimentary jewelry and what some believe to be tools buried with them. Were these items intended to prepare the dead for the afterlife? Were they a way of honoring the dead in the belief that they lived on? We can't be sure, but many believe that these practices reflect a belief of the earliest humans in life after death.

Nearly every ancient culture had some ritual for marking death, and most held a hope that human existence did not end with death. I traveled to Egypt recently and explored the Valley of the Kings, walking through the tombs of the pharaohs who ruled over Egypt in the second half of the second millennium before Christ. It is clear that the Egyptians believed that their leaders survived death and that the pharaohs anticipated a life to come.

Likewise Stonehenge in southern England bears witness to the hope of people living four thousand to five thousand years ago that something of us survives the grave. Scholars are still not completely certain about the meaning of this amazing monument, but the burials nearby appear to point to the hope of these ancient people that death was not the end for their loved ones.

Death is the one shared experience of all human beings. We will bury people we love. We will wrestle with our own mortality. And, like all people who have gone before us, we will wonder and perhaps hope that there is something beyond this life.

Though the ancient Hebrews did not speak a lot about surviving after death, they did speak about the realm of the dead, a place they called Sheol (discussed in Chapter 2), where it appears they believed the dead continue in some state. Toward the end of the Old Testament period, we find the beginning of a more expanded understanding of the afterlife.

In the period between the Old and New Testaments, the idea of the resurrection of the dead and an afterlife became more prominent. The following diagram shows how some Jews in the time of Jesus may have imagined the afterlife and what would follow. It captures the ideas I first mentioned in Chapter 2 as we considered Jesus' descent to the dead. It helps us make sense of some things Jesus taught and some things the apostles wrote. (As I noted in Chapter 2, Jesus' parable of the rich man and Lazarus draws upon this idea, as does his promise to the thief on the cross that "today you will be with me in paradise." Likewise it helps us understand Paul's teaching about the Second Coming of Christ.)

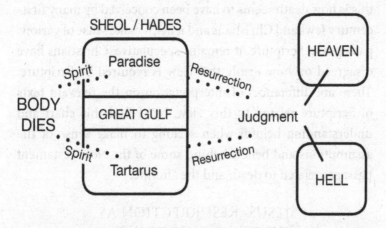

As shown in the diagram, the realm of the dead, called Sheol but also known as Hades, had two distinct areas: Paradise, the place of the righteous dead; and Tartarus (sometimes called Gehenna), the place of the wicked dead. Yet consignment of the dead to Paradise or Tartarus was not final. At some point the dead would be raised and a final judgment would take place. Jesus, Paul, and some of the other apostles taught that there would be a final judgment, at which time those in both realms of the dead would be brought before the judgment seat of Christ. Some would be granted eternal life in heaven, receiving a new resurrection body, while the others would be cast out into a realm of "weeping and gnashing of teeth" (Luke 13:28 NRSV).

According to this view, after death both the righteous and the unrighteous enter the realm of the dead—the righteous to Paradise, the unrighteous to Tartarus or Gehenna. They have not faced the final judgment. The dead have not received their resurrection bodies, but they are very much alive. While this is how death seems to have been conceived by many first-century Jews and Christians and it helps make sense of various passages in Scripture, it remains speculative. Christians have disagreed on how firmly this view is required by Scripture. There are differences of interpretation on the relevant texts of Scripture related to this view, but I find this chart and understanding helpful when seeking to make sense of the assumptions and beliefs behind some of the New Testament passages related to death and the afterlife.

JESUS' RESURRECTION AS GOD'S RESPONSE TO DEATH

To remind you of what we discussed in Chapter 2, Christians believe that in Jesus' death and resurrection, God gave a definitive answer to the existential questions of death and life beyond death. Clearly Jesus was crucified, dead, and buried. His friends grieved and mourned his death. But those same friends claimed that on Sunday morning, after his death on Friday, Jesus stepped out of the tomb.

These men and women claimed that they had seen him, eaten with him, touched him, and been taught by him for forty days after his death. The tomb in which he had been buried was empty; people could go and see it. Jesus' disciples, who, fearing for their lives, had gone into hiding after his death, boldly stepped into the streets to proclaim that he had risen. In the years following, people such as Paul, who had initially rejected Christianity and had even persecuted Christians, claimed to have had encounters, visions, and profound experiences of the risen Christ. Once again, in the late 50s, Paul wrote of Jesus that "he appeared to more than five hundred brothers and sisters at once—most of them are still alive to this day" (1 Corinthians 15:6).

With this confidence, Paul could affirm that for him there was no question that we survive death, and he could write, quoting Isaiah 25:8, "Death has been swallowed up by a victory" (1 Corinthians 15:54). Later Paul wrote, "We know that if the earthly tent we live in is destroyed, we have a building from God, an eternal house in heaven, not built by human hands" (2 Corinthians 5:1 NIV). It's what Jesus meant when he said, "I am the resurrection and the life. Whoever believes in me will live, even though they die. Everyone who lives and believes in me will never die" (John 11:25-26).

We believe in life beyond death because Jesus rose from the dead, the disciples bore witness to it, and those who came later had profound experiences with the risen Christ. Jesus' death and resurrection were, in part, God's way of speaking to the deepest and most fundamental human crisis: death.

I love that phrase in Scripture, included in the Creed: "On the third day he rose again." As important as Jesus' death is for Christians, it was his resurrection that demonstrated his triumph over evil, hate, sin, and death. As Jesus said in John, "Because I live, you will live too" (John 14:19).

Once again, the existentialist theologian Paul Tillich offered an important word when he wrote, "The face of every man shows the trace of the presence of death in his life, of his fear of death, of his courage toward death, and of his resignation to death. This frightful presence of death subjects man to bondage and servitude all his life."[1] The resurrection of Jesus from the dead is God's answer to the "frightful presence of death," and in one great act on Easter morning Christ liberated believers from death's "bondage and servitude."

That first Easter, the disciples remained in hiding. They had not yet seen Jesus. They did not expect his resurrection from the grave. When the women came announcing that Jesus had been raised, the disciples thought the women were out of their minds. Then suddenly he appeared among them, saying, "Peace be with you" (John 20:21). In this simple statement Jesus was expressing, in part, what his resurrection and the promise of eternal life mean to us. By conquering death, Jesus addressed our fear and uncertainty and offered his first disciples, and us, a peace that sustains us even in the face of great tragedy and pain.

I'm reminded of Thomas Dorsey, one of the greats of African American gospel music. Just days after losing his first wife, Nettie, and their son during childbirth, Dorsey wrote the beloved hymn "Precious Lord, Take My Hand."

Through the storm, through the night, lead me on to
    the light
Take my hand, precious Lord, lead me home.[2]

It was Dorsey's faith that Christ lives, that he walks with us, that there is a resurrection of the body and a life everlasting, that made it possible for him to write those words just days after laying his wife and infant son to rest.

THE RETURN OF CHRIST

Before we consider what the Creed means by the resurrection of the body, we might take a moment to consider an idea mentioned earlier in the Creed—namely, that Christ "will come again to judge the living and the dead." Christians from the first apostles on have anticipated that Christ will one day return and bring to an end history as we know it. This is an affirmation we find throughout the New Testament. We have Paul affirming the return of Christ with these words, among the earliest in the New Testament:

> *The Lord himself will come down from*
> *heaven, with a loud command, with the voice*
> *of the archangel and with the trumpet call*
> *of God, and the dead in Christ will rise first.*
> *After that, we who are still alive and are left*
> *will be caught up together with them in the*
> *clouds to meet the Lord in the air.*
> *(1 Thessalonians 4:16-17 NIV)*

How and when the Lord will return is unclear in Scripture. Less clear still is how to interpret the various passages that seem to point to it. It appears that the earliest Christians believed he would return within their lifetime. By the end of the New Testament period, the author of Second Peter reaffirmed Christ's return but gave a nod to the delay in his return when he wrote:

> *Don't let it escape your notice, dear friends,*
> *that with the Lord a single day is like a*

Creed

*thousand years and a thousand years are like
a single day. The Lord isn't slow to keep his
promise, as some think of slowness, but he is
patient toward you, not wanting anyone to
perish but all to change their hearts and lives.
But the day of the Lord will come like a thief.
On that day the heavens will pass away with a
dreadful noise, the elements will be consumed
by fire, and the earth and all the works done
on it will be exposed.*

*(2 Peter 3:8-10)**

Throughout history, every generation has interpreted some
of the Old Testament books such as Daniel and Ezekiel, along
with portions of New Testament books such as Matthew, First
and Second Thessalonians, and Revelation, as road maps to
the end times, and some readers have correlated those end
times with events in their own time, thus predicting Christ's
imminent return. In the last two hundred years this has
happened again and again. The Seventh-day Adventists, for
example, had their beginning in the teaching of a man who
believed Jesus was returning in 1843 or 1844. The Jehovah's
Witnesses started with a man who believed Jesus would
launch his kingdom on earth in 1914.

In 1970 a book came out by a man named Hal Lindsey, titled
The Late Great Planet Earth. It strongly suggested that Jesus

---

* Most mainline scholars believe that Second Peter was likely the last book of the New
Testament written, dating to the end of the first century or the first half of the second
century, if not later. By this time it had become important for the author to address
the delayed return of Christ.

would return by 1988, largely based upon the reestablishment of the State of Israel in 1948. The book sold thirty million copies and in 1979 was made into a movie narrated by Orson Welles. Since then, there has been no shortage of predictions about the return of Christ: something like fifty different dates have been named by various Christian pastors since 1980. In 2014 and 2015, several authors sold millions of books hinting strongly that the end times were coming, due to a tetrad of lunar eclipses. During a lunar eclipse the moon appears to be red and is sometimes referred to as a "blood moon."

These authors cited Joel 2:31: "The sun will be turned to darkness, and the moon to blood before the great and dreadful day of the LORD comes." They suggested that the end was near, yet left themselves a wide opening in the event that nothing happened. Millions of people around the world who had read or heard their predictions waited to see if the end would come on the date they had suggested, September 27, 2015.

Of course, nothing happened. This group of end-times prophets is like many others in the last two hundred years who wrongly predicted dates for the return of Christ.

Having said that, the point of the biblical texts (and the Creed's affirmation) that one day Christ "will come again to judge the living and the dead" was to challenge Christians to be ready on that day when Christ does return, whether in a glorious second coming or at our death. The words concerning the second coming have served to encourage believers who might be facing adversity and suffering. In reciting those words, believers could have faith that, regardless of the difficulty they might be facing, the day was coming when there would be no more sorrow, pain, or suffering and when Christ would make all things right.

I do believe that one day Christ will return, but I don't spend time pondering when it will be, and I recognize that *that* second coming could be thousands of years after he returns for me at the hour of my death. One point of teaching about the return of Christ is that we should always be ready to meet Christ. And we do that by trusting daily in his grace, seeking to follow him, and trusting the Spirit to lead us. A second and perhaps larger point is that the world will not continue as it is forever. Ultimately evil, suffering, sin, and death will be completely defeated on the day of Christ's return.

WHAT IS HEAVEN LIKE?

So, Christians trust that our lives continue beyond death. We believe that Christ will return for us at our death, and most take seriously the idea that one day Christ will bring an end to the world as we know it. But the question many want to know is, what is heaven like?

Paul reminds us that *"God has prepared things for those who love him that no eye has seen, or ear has heard, or that haven't crossed the mind of any human being"* (1 Corinthians 2:9). Since heaven can't be imagined or described, the biblical authors must resort to analogies based on human experience.

Jesus uses one analogy that we find in Isaiah and Revelation: heaven is like a wedding reception. When our older daughter married several years ago, I had the joy of both walking her down the aisle and then co-officiating. I held back tears of joy as I led the service. But while the service was the most "meaning-full" part of the day, it was at the reception where the fun really began. All the people who were most important in their lives and ours had come to celebrate. There was food, toasting, music, and dancing. LaVon and I laughed and danced and celebrated all night long with our children and friends. And when we got home late that night and collapsed into bed, completely exhausted, LaVon turned to me and said, "That was the best night of our lives!" And she was right. When Jesus compared heaven to a wedding reception, I believe that's what he meant. That's how I picture heaven.

The Book of Isaiah gives us a glimpse of God's heavenly kingdom that inspired the writer of Revelation centuries later. It captures this idea of heaven as a great feast.

> On this mountain the LORD of hosts will make
> for all peoples
>   a feast of rich food, a feast of well-aged wines,
>   of rich food filled with marrow, of well-
>   aged wines strained clear.
> And he will destroy on this mountain
>   the shroud that is cast over all peoples,
>   the sheet that is spread over all nations;
>   he will swallow up death forever.
> Then the Lord God will wipe away the tears
> from all faces.
>
> *(Isaiah 25:6-8 NRSV)*

Beyond these kinds of images, we don't have a great deal of detail about heaven. Whatever words we find in Scripture about pearly gates and streets of gold are simply ways of saying that if you take the most beautiful things on this earth, heaven is even more glorious.

But for many Christians, the most comforting thing that can be said about heaven is what was captured in a story about a man who lived alone and was nearing death. This was in the days before cars, and the doctor arrived in his horse-drawn carriage to check on his patient. The doctor brought his dog along, leaving the dog outside on the front step as he entered the house. The doctor sat down beside the man, took his vital signs, and then told the man that the end was near. The man asked, "Doc, what is death like? What's on the other side?" At that moment the doctor's dog began to whimper and scratch at the front door. The doctor said, "Do you hear that? That's my dog. He's never been in your house. He doesn't know what it's like in here. What he knows is that his master is on the other side of that door, and if his master is in here, it must be OK. Our Master is on the other side of death's door."

THE RESURRECTION OF THE BODY

I want to return to this odd phrase in the Creed, "the resurrection of the body." I must admit that I'm a bit perplexed by it. I believe in the resurrection of the soul, that after death we live on. But the resurrection of the body is more challenging to understand.*

Does the phrase mean that this body we have will be resurrected? How is that possible given that our bodies decompose, starting within minutes of our death? In the first century, bodies were buried in tombs, and within a year or

---

* Undoubtedly some reading this section will refer me to N. T. Wright's important work on this question. I've read both what he's written and what he's said in interviews on the subject. I agree with much of what he says, but I still have a few questions. What I've written is my attempt to make sense of the "resurrection of the body."

two the flesh was completely consumed, at which point the bones were cleaned and placed in a box called an ossuary. What was to be resurrected? Was it the bones? What about people who died at sea? What about people who were burned, as some of the first Christians were by Nero to entertain his dinner guests? Presumably the bones of these people were completely destroyed.

A camera was placed inside what is thought to be Paul's tomb in Rome, and it showed that after two thousand years, only small bone fragments remained. So is it really these bodies that are resurrected? I hope not. I've enjoyed this body, but it's been prone to sickness, I constantly struggle to keep my weight down, my hair is thinning, my skin is wrinkling, and I'm only fifty-two! And if somehow this body is resurrected, at what age is it resurrected? Will I see my grandparents as I knew them, in their seventies or eighties, or will they look the way they did in their twenties or thirties—in which case, will I recognize them?

When we read about Jesus' resurrection, we learn that his body had changed. Mary Magdalene, the first to see him, did not recognize him and thought he was the gardener. The two disciples walking to Emmaus thought he was a stranger. When his followers gathered around him just before he ascended to heaven, some of them did not recognize his appearance. Yes, he had the ability to eat, and there were scars from his crucifixion on his hands and side. He had flesh they could touch. But he also walked through walls. These appearances by Jesus may give us pieces of a puzzle regarding what our life in heaven will be like.

Paul offered an answer in a letter to the Corinthians:

> *A rotting body is put into the ground, but*
> *what is raised won't ever decay. It's degraded*
> *when it's put into the ground, but it's raised in*
> *glory. It's weak when it's put into the ground,*
> *but it's raised in power. It's a physical body*
> *when it's put into the ground, but it's raised as*
> *a spiritual body....*
>
> *And when the rotting body has been clothed in*
> *what can't decay, and the dying body has been*
> *clothed in what can't die, then this statement*
> *in scripture will happen:*
>
> *"Death has been swallowed up by a victory."*
>   *(1 Corinthians 15:42-44, 54)*

God does not require what was rotting in the ground to give you a new body, but somehow, according to Paul, your "spiritual body" is connected to that fleshly body. The resurrection of the body, in other words, is not like a bad zombie movie. The bodies of most Christians throughout history have been completely absorbed back into the earth. But here's where modern DNA work is interesting. We now know that our physical bodies are the result of an amazingly complex sequence of nucleic acids called DNA. Essentially this is our software, and it's different in every individual. Surely God, who wrote the software that makes up life, has our DNA sequenced and "on file" and can use it to create whatever kind of "heavenly body" God intends. He does not need our mortal body to raise us from the dead.

What I love about this idea of the resurrection of the body is that we will not be a disembodied spirit after death, but instead we will have a glorious body that isn't subject to disease. No more aches and pains. If Jesus' appearances following his resurrection are any guide, we'll be able to touch, feel, eat, drink, see, and be. Yet our body will be different from anything we've experienced on this side of eternity—a glorious body by which those who have known us in the past will know us in heaven. Christians have often seen in the caterpillar and the butterfly a picture of the connection between this earthly body and the heavenly body.

Drawing upon the passage from Isaiah I cited earlier, the author of Revelation wrote that in the eternal Jerusalem, the heavenly kingdom,

> *"God himself will be with them as their God.*
> *He will wipe away every tear from their*
> *eyes. Death will be no more. There will be no*
> *mourning, crying, or pain anymore, for the*
> *former things have passed away." Then the one*
> *seated on the throne said, "Look! I'm making*
> *all things new."*
>
> (Revelation 21:3-5)

In the three weeks during which I was completing the final revisions of the book you are holding, I visited two people in hospice, officiated or assisted in the funerals of four people, and lost my great-aunt. The question of death and resurrection is not some abstract concept about something far in the future. It is something these people and their family and friends wanted to know about here and now. And what we believe about death affects both how we face our own death and how we grieve the loss of those we love.

I sat with an eighty-seven-year-old man named Ben, who by the time you read this book will have passed. He's been a civic leader, and a personal mentor and friend. As a young man he played on the same baseball team with Mickey Mantle. Years later, as a businessman and community leader, he shaped an entire county. Ben got a bit choked up as we talked about his life and his impending death. But he also had a confidence that death was not the end. He was not afraid to die and hoped to make every day count until he breathed his last.

I sat with Julie just days before she died at the age of fifty-three from a cancer the doctors could not beat. She served with me on our staff at the church. Her son and daughter-in-law are both pastors and are expecting their first child. Shortly before her death, Julie wrote,

> My physical health is declining more quickly, but joy and peace are close at hand.... Thanks to God, I am strong spiritually and emotionally, but the body is frail. I have today...just as I have had today every day of this journey on earth. Today I smiled at the expanding belly on sweet Katherine as she lovingly grows my next grandbaby, I listened to my daughter and granddaughter rehearse an amazing song for my funeral, and I held my son's hand as he prayed for me. It was a beautiful day.

At her funeral, though her death was untimely, there was laughter and joy as people remembered her love of life, her steadfast faith, and the hope that she had that she would see them all again one day. We celebrated her life and the hope that Christians confess in the Creed—the hope of the resurrection of the body and the life everlasting.

Christ's resurrection, and his promise that we will be raised, is God's answer to the questions every human asks about death and the afterlife. I end every funeral I preach in the same way that I end every Easter sermon: "People ask me from time to time if I really believe that Jesus rose from the dead and has gone on to prepare a place for us—that death doesn't have the final word in our lives, and that because he lives we will live also. And my answer is always the same: 'I not only believe in it; I'm counting on it.'"

WORDS TO LIVE BY

I want to end our study with a story that helped me understand the importance of the Apostles' Creed in the Christian spiritual life and that helped me see, once again, the importance of the gospel.

On a Sunday morning some years ago, just after I sat down having preached the sermon, one of our associate pastors passed me a note. I opened it and read, "Doug and Hannah's son George has just died in an accident. They are on their way to the airport and can be reached at this number tonight." Their son George had just graduated from college. He had taken a hiking trip and, while hiking, had lost his footing and slipped to his death.

When I finally reached Doug by phone later that night I could hear the pain in his voice. I told him I wished I could be there with him, just to hold him. I told him how terribly sorry I was for George's death and how I wished I had the right words to say that would make it all OK. I'll never forget what he said to me: "Adam, there's only one thing that's holding me together right now. It's a set of words I memorized when I was a child in church."

I asked, "What words are those, Doug?"

He answered, "I believe in God, the Father Almighty, creator of heaven and earth. I believe in Jesus Christ, his only Son, our Lord, who was conceived by the Holy Spirit, born of the Virgin Mary, suffered under Pontius Pilate, was crucified, died, and was buried; he descended to the dead. On the third day he rose again; he ascended into heaven, is seated at the right hand of the Father, and will come again to judge the living and the dead. I believe in the Holy Spirit, the holy catholic church, the communion of saints, the forgiveness of sins," and then he spoke with determination and strength, "the resurrection of the body, and the life everlasting."

"Pastor, that's all that's holding me together right now."

That's what the Creed, and the gospel it bears witness to, is meant to do. It helps us remember God's answers to the deepest wounds, longings, and questions of our hearts. It reminds us of what is true. It captures many of the foundational convictions upon which our lives are built. And it gives us hope.

It's been said that what you believe about death changes how you face life. It leads us to face death with courage and to take risks we might not otherwise take. It puts this earthly life and what we do with it in perspective. And it helps us to grieve as those who have hope.

AN INVITATION

In the end I cannot prove to you that there is a God. I look at the beauty of creation, the vastness of space, the amazing genetic software that makes us what we are, and I see the evidence of a creative, magnificent God. Others look at all of this and believe that it sprang forth out of nothing, on its own, and marvel at a self-made universe. We look at the same evidence and draw different conclusions.

Some read the story of Jesus and see the most remarkable human being who ever lived. They believe the accounts of the first-century witnesses who knew him and of those whose lives were changed by him. They pledge to follow him, and as they do they find their lives changed for the better. Others read his story and wonder whether he really lived, or, if they accept him as a historical figure, whether his early followers, in their devotion, created elaborate stories about the miracles he wrought and his resurrection from the dead. Once more we see the same data but reach different conclusions.

Some claim to have experienced God's Spirit guiding them, speaking to them, comforting, nudging, leading, forming, and shaping them. Their family and friends often witness that their faith has made them more authentically human—more loving, patient, compassionate, and kind. Others believe these feelings reflect the power of the human mind to fabricate experiences that match what it believes in. Again, the same data, different conclusions.

And some believe that Jesus spoke the truth when he said there is life beyond death. Some claim to have had near-death or post-death experiences that testify to this. They believe that this life is only the preface to a great adventure that begins in our passing. Even though, in the words of the psalmist, they "walk through the valley of the shadow of death," they fear no evil, and they trust that, at their passing, they will "dwell in the house of the LORD forever" (Psalm 23:4, 6 NKJV). They live life and face death with hope. Others believe that when we die we die, we cease to exist, and that all the talk of an afterlife is only wishful thinking. They hear the same stories, read the same accounts in the Gospels, but don't believe them to be true.

In the end we make a choice to believe. That's how the Creed begins, *credo* in Latin: I choose to believe these truths; I choose to build my life upon this foundation; I have decided that if I must take a leap of faith, I'll take this leap of faith rather than the other.

Here's my invitation to you: if you are not yet a Christian, I invite you to believe—to trust in this set of truths that Christians have been professing for nearly two thousand years. You don't need to have it all figured out. You can have your questions and your doubts; God knows I do. But you can still make the decision that you believe—you trust that God exists, that God came to us in Jesus, and that, by means of the Holy Spirit, God is as close as the air you breathe. I invite you to begin to pray and speak to God—Father, Son, and Holy Spirit. Prayer is simply conversation with God. And I invite you to read the Bible, starting with the Gospels, looking to see what they teach you about Jesus, and what Jesus teaches you about God. Finally, I invite you to find a church—one that will help you grow in your faith, and whose members will act with love and grace and will welcome you.

If you are a Christian, I invite you to long for a deeper love of God and neighbor, to trust God with your life, to seek to follow Jesus more fully than ever, and to invite the Holy Spirit to daily fill you and to work in and through you. And I encourage you, if you don't have one already, to find a church where you can get involved, grow in your faith, and join others in serving. This Christian journey is good. It is life-giving. And, as we've seen, it is filled with hope.

Now I invite you to join me in this historic confession of the Christian faith, saying, and praying, these words:

> *I believe in God, the Father Almighty,*
> *   creator of heaven and earth.*

> *I believe in Jesus Christ, his only Son, our Lord,*
> *   who was conceived by the Holy Spirit,*
> *   born of the Virgin Mary,*
> *   suffered under Pontius Pilate,*
> *   was crucified, died, and was buried;*
> *   he descended to the dead.*
> *   On the third day he rose again;*
> *   he ascended into heaven,*
> *   is seated at the right hand of the Father,*
> *   and will come again to judge the living and*
> *   the dead.*

> *I believe in the Holy Spirit,*
> *   the holy catholic church,*
> *   the communion of saints,*
> *   the forgiveness of sins,*
> *   the resurrection of the body,*
> *   and the life everlasting. Amen.*[3]

Creed

And now you might pray these words:

O God, I trust that you exist and that the wonders of our universe are all your handiwork. Thank you for creating this planet on which we live with its capacity to sustain life. Thank you for creating human beings in your image and for making it possible for us to understand and acknowledge you as our Creator. Thank you for caring about us and for us.

Jesus Christ, thank you for the truth you came to reveal, the life you came to give us, the death you suffered for us, and for the resurrection by which you conquered evil, hate, sin, and death. I trust you as my Savior. Help me to follow you daily as my Lord.

Come, Holy Spirit, fill my heart. Form me and shape me as a potter shapes the clay. Transform my heart, sanctify me, and make me the person you intend me to be. Help me to love and to bear your fruit in my life.

Thank you, O God—Father, Son, and Holy Spirit. All that I am, I offer to you. Help me to live the words of the Creed and to incorporate their meaning into my daily life.

In Jesus' name,

Amen.

Appendix

THE CREEDS OF THE CHURCH

The word *creed* comes from the Latin *credo*, which means "I believe." The earliest Christian creeds were summaries of belief, simple statements of faith confessing Jesus as Lord. Today, Christians across the globe recite creeds to reaffirm their most basic tenets of faith.

What follows are some of the earliest creeds of Christianity. They begin with the very brief confession "Jesus is Lord" found in the Apostle Paul's letters. Paul notes in Romans 10:9, "If you confess with your mouth 'Jesus is Lord' and in your heart you have faith that God raised him from the dead, you will be saved."

By the mid-second century, if not before, the Greek word for fish, IXTHUS or ICHTHUS, was thought to have been adopted by some Christians as an acronym summarizing what Christians believed about Jesus. Around this same time the Old Roman Symbol, an early and fairly complete version of the Apostles' Creed, was developed as a summary statement of Christian faith.

The Apostles' Creed, from the fourth century, earned its name from the legend, since shown to be incorrect, that the apostles themselves wrote the creed on the tenth day after Christ's ascension. This version of today's creed was often used to teach the faith to converts in preparation for baptism. In the early Roman church, baptism often occurred during the Easter vigil, making our modern-day Lenten season a meaningful time to study the Apostles' Creed.

From the fourth century on, additional creeds were developed in response to theological debates in the church or to clarify what the church believed. However, as you can see on the following pages, the primary focus remained on Christology, what the church believed about Jesus.

ROMANS 10:9 AND 1 CORINTHIANS 12:3 (1ST CENTURY)

"Jesus is Lord"

IXTHUS (2ND CENTURY)

Jesus Christ, God's Son, the Savior

THE OLD ROMAN SYMBOL (2ND OR 3RD CENTURY)

I believe in God the Father almighty;
and in Christ Jesus His only Son, our Lord,
Who was born from the Holy Spirit and the
Virgin Mary,
Who under Pontius Pilate was crucified and buried,
on the third day rose again from the dead,
ascended to heaven,
sits at the right hand of the Father,
whence He will come to judge the living
and the dead;
and in the Holy Spirit,
the holy Church,
the remission of sins,
the resurrection of the flesh
(the life everlasting).[1]

THE APOSTLES' CREED
(LATIN – 4TH CENTURY)

Credo in Deum Patrem *omnipotentem;*
Creatorem cæli et terræ.

Et in Jesum Christum, *Filium ejus unicum,*
Dominum nostrum; qui conceptus est de
Spiritu Sancto, natus ex Maria virgine; passus
sub Pontio Pilato, crucifixus, mortuus, et
sepultus; descendit ad inferna;* tertia die
resurrexit a mortuis; ascendit ad cælos; sedet
ad dexteram Dei Patris omnipotentis; inde
venturus (est) judicare vivos et mortuos.

Credo in Spiritum Sanctum; *sanctam*
ecclesiam catholicam; sanctorum
communionem; remissionem peccatorum;
carnis resurrectionem; vitam æternam. Amen.[2]

---

* Some Latin texts use *ad inferos* which translates as "to the inhabitants of the spirit-world."

THE APOSTLES' CREED
(4TH CENTURY)

I believe in God, the Father Almighty,
creator of heaven and earth.

I believe in Jesus Christ, his only Son, our Lord,
who was conceived by the Holy Spirit,
born of the Virgin Mary,
suffered under Pontius Pilate,
was crucified, died, and was buried;
he descended to the dead.
On the third day he rose again;
he ascended into heaven,
is seated at the right hand of the Father,
and will come again to judge the living
and the dead.

I believe in the Holy Spirit,
the holy catholic* church,
the communion of saints,
the forgiveness of sins,
the resurrection of the body,
and the life everlasting. Amen.[3]

---

* universal

THE NICENE CREED
(A.D. 325)

*We believe in one God, the Father Almighty,
Maker of all things visible and invisible.*

*And in one Lord Jesus Christ, the Son of God,
begotten of the Father [the only-begotten; that
is, of the essence of the Father, God of God],
Light of Light, very God of very God, begotten,
not made, being of one substance with the
Father; by whom all things were made [both
in heaven and on earth]; who for us men,
and for our salvation, came down and was
incarnate and was made man; he suffered,
and the third day he rose again, ascended into
heaven; from thence he shall come to judge the
quick and the dead.*

And in the Holy Ghost.[4]

THE NICENE CREED
(AS AMENDED IN A.D. 381)

We believe in one God,
the Father, the Almighty,
maker of heaven and earth,
of all that is, seen and unseen.

We believe in one Lord, Jesus Christ,
the only Son of God,
eternally begotten of the Father,
God from God, Light from Light,
true God from true God,
begotten, not made,
of one Being with the Father;
through him all things were made.
For us and for our salvation
he came down from heaven,
was incarnate of the Holy Spirit and the Virgin Mary
and became truly human.
For our sake he was crucified under Pontius Pilate;
he suffered death and was buried.
On the third day he rose again
in accordance with the Scriptures;
he ascended into heaven
and is seated at the right hand of the Father.
He will come again in glory
to judge the living and the dead,
and his kingdom will have no end.

Creed

We believe in the Holy Spirit, the Lord, the giver of life,
who proceeds from the Father and the Son,
who with the Father and the Son
   is worshiped and glorified,
who has spoken through the prophets.
We believe in one holy catholic *and apostolic church.
We acknowledge one baptism
   for the forgiveness of sins.
We look for the resurrection of the dead,
   and the life of the world to come. Amen.[5]

---

* universal

THE CHALCEDONIAN CREED
(A.D. 451)

We, then, following the holy Fathers, all with one consent, teach men to confess one and the same Son, our Lord Jesus Christ, the same perfect in Godhead and also perfect in manhood; truly God and truly man, of a reasonable [rational] soul and body; consubstantial [coessential] with the Father according to the Godhead, and consubstantial with us according to the Manhood; in all things like unto us, without sin; begotten before all ages of the Father according to the Godhead, and in these latter days, for us and for our salvation, born of the Virgin Mary, the Mother of God, according to the Manhood; one and the same Christ, Son, Lord, only begotten, to be acknowledged in two natures, inconfusedly, unchangeably, indivisibly, inseparably; the distinction of natures being by no means taken away by the union, but rather the property of each nature being preserved, and concurring in one Person and one Subsistence, not parted or divided into two persons, but one and the same Son, and only begotten, God the Word, the Lord Jesus Christ, as the prophets from the beginning [have declared] concerning him, and the Lord Jesus Christ himself has taught us, and the Creed of the holy Fathers has handed down to us.[6]

THE ATHANASIAN CREED
(6TH - 8TH CENTURY)

1. *Whosoever will be saved: before all things it is necessary that he hold the Catholic Faith:*
2. *Which Faith except every one do keep whole and undefiled: without doubt he shall perish everlastingly.*
3. *And the Catholic Faith is this: That we worship one God in Trinity, and Trinity in Unity;*
4. *Neither confounding the Persons: nor dividing the Substance [Essence].*
5. *For there is one Person of the Father: another of the Son: and another of the Holy Ghost.*
6. *But the Godhead of the Father, of the Son, and of the Holy Ghost, is all one: the Glory equal, the Majesty coeternal.*
7. *Such as the Father is: such is the Son: and such is the Holy Ghost.*
8. *The Father uncreate [uncreated]: the Son uncreate [uncreated]: and the Holy Ghost uncreate [uncreated].*
9. *The Father incomprehensible [unlimited]: the Son incomprehensible [unlimited]: and the Holy Ghost incomprehensible [unlimited, or infinite].*
10. *The Father eternal: the Son eternal: and the Holy Ghost eternal.*
11. *And yet they are not three eternals: but one eternal.*

12. *As also there are not three uncreated: nor three incomprehensibles [infinites], but one uncreated: and one incomprehensible [infinite].*

13. *So likewise the Father is Almighty: the Son Almighty: and the Holy Ghost Almighty.*

14. *And yet they are not three Almighties: but one Almighty.*

15. *So the Father is God: the Son is God: and the Holy Ghost is God.*

16. *And yet they are not three Gods: but one God.*

17. *So likewise the Father is Lord: the Son Lord: and the Holy Ghost Lord.*

18. *And yet not three Lords: but one Lord.*

19. *For like as we are compelled by the Christian verity: to acknowledge every Person by himself to be God and Lord:*

20. *So are we forbidden by the Catholic Religion: to say, There be [are] three Gods, or three Lords.*

21. *The Father is made of none: neither created, nor begotten.*

22. *The Son is of the Father alone: not made, nor created: but begotten.*

23. *The Holy Ghost is of the Father and of the Son: neither made, nor created, nor begotten: but proceeding.*

24. *So there is one Father, not three Fathers: one Son, not three Sons: one Holy Ghost, not three Holy Ghosts.*

25. *And in this Trinity none is afore, or after another: none is greater, or less than another [there is nothing before, or after: nothing greater or less].*

26. *But the whole three Persons are coeternal, and coequal.*

27. *So that in all things, as aforesaid: the Unity in Trinity, and the Trinity in Unity, is to be worshiped.*

28. *He therefore that will be saved, must [let him] thus think of the Trinity.*

29. *Furthermore it is necessary to everlasting salvation: that he also believe rightly [faithfully] the Incarnation of our Lord Jesus Christ.*

30. *For the right Faith is, that we believe and confess: that our Lord Jesus Christ, the Son of God, is God and Man;*

31. *God, of the Substance [Essence] of the Father; begotten before the worlds: and Man, of the Substance [Essence] of his Mother, born in the world.*

32. *Perfect God: and perfect Man, of a reasonable soul and human flesh subsisting.*

33. *Equal to the Father, as touching his Godhead: and inferior to the Father as touching his Manhood.*

34. *Who although he be [is] God and Man; yet he is not two, but one Christ.*

35. *One; not by conversion of the Godhead into flesh: but by taking [assumption] of the Manhood into God.*

36. *One altogether; not by confusion of Substance [Essence]: but by unity of Person.*

37. *For as the reasonable soul and flesh is one man: so God and Man is one Christ;*

38. *Who suffered for our salvation: descended into hell [Hades, spirit-world]: rose again the third day from the dead.*

39. *He ascended into heaven, he sitteth on the right hand of the Father God [God the Father] Almighty.*

40. *From whence [thence] he shall come to judge the quick and the dead.*

41. *At whose coming all men shall rise again with their bodies;*

42. *And shall give account for their own works.*

43. *And they that have done good shall go into life everlasting: and they that have done evil, into everlasting fire.*

44. *This is the Catholic Faith: which except a man believe faithfully [truly and firmly], he can not be saved.*[7]

NOTES

1. "The Apostles' Creed, Ecumenical Version," *The United Methodist Hymnal* (Nashville: The United Methodist Publishing House), #882.
2. *Merriam Webster Dictionary Online*, s.v. "creed." accessed August 4, 2016, http://www.merriam-webster.com/dictionary/creed.

INTRODUCTION

1. George Sylvester Viereck, "What Life Means to Einstein: An interview by George Sylvester Viereck," *The Saturday Evening Post* (Indianapolis:IN), October 6, 1929, 117. http://www.saturdayeveningpost.com/wp-content/uploads/satevepost/what_life_means_to_einstein.pdf

CHAPTER 1

1. Michael Brooks and Helen Philips, "Beyond Belief: In place of God," *New Scientist*, November 15, 2006. https://www.newscientist.com/article/mg19225780-142-beyond-belief-in-place-of-god/.
2. Walter Isaacson, *Einstein: His Life and Universe* (New York: Simon and Schuster, 39).
3. Max Planck, "Das Wesen der Materie" [The Nature of Matter], speech at Florence, Italy (1944), from Archiv zur Geschichte der Max-Planck-Gesellschaft, Abt. Va, Rep. 11 Planck, Nr. 1797.
4. Lawrence M. Krauss, *A Universe from Nothing* (New York: Free Press), 18.
5. Richard Dawkins, *The God Delusion* (Boston: Houghton Mifflin, 2006), 113, where Dawkins then turns the analogy to say that if this is the likelihood of life emerging on earth, what is the likelihood of God emerging at all. By the way, Hoyle didn't believe in God either, but believed life must have started somewhere in space because it could not have spontaneously generated here on earth.

CHAPTER 2

1. Dawkins noted in an interview as part of John Harris's National Conversation series for *The Guardian* (October 24, 2011) that "Jesus was a great moral teacher" and he went on to say, "Somebody as intelligent as Jesus would have been an atheist if he had known what we know today." https://www.theguardian.com/science/audio/2011/oct/24/john-harris -national-conversations-podcast-richard-dawkins.

2. Bart Ehrman, *Did Jesus Exist?* (New York: HarperCollins, 2012), 339.

3. Ker Than, "'Virgin Birth' Seen in Wild Snakes, Even When Males Are Available," *National Geographic News*, September 15, 2012, http://news.nationalgeographic.com/news/2012/09/120914-virgin -birth-parthenogenesis-snakes-science-biology-letters/.

4. James S. Stewart, *Thine Is the Kingdom* (New York: Scribner's, 1956), 22.

5. "The Nicene Creed," *The United Methodist Hymnal*, #880.

6. Richard Dawkins, *The Selfish Gene 30th Anniversary Edition* (New York: Oxford University Press Inc., 2006), xxi.

7. Jaroslav Pelikan, introduction to *Jesus Through the Centuries: His Place in the History of Culture* (New Haven: Yale University Press, 1985), 1.

8. See Roger Olson's post about these now famous words of Barth's: http://www.patheos.com/blogs/rogereolson/2013/01/did-karl-barth -really-say-jesus-loves-me-this-i-know/.

CHAPTER 3

1. Jack Levison, *Fresh Air* (Brewster, Mass.: Paraclete, 2012), introduction, Kindle edition.

2. Reginald Heber, "Holy, Holy, Holy! Lord God Almighty," *The United Methodist Hymnal*, #64.

CHAPTER 4

1. Henri de Lubac, *Catholicism: Christ and the Common Destiny of Man* (San Francisco: Ignatius Press, 1988), 76.

2. Charles Wesley, "Glory to God, and Praise and Love" *The United Methodist Hymnal*, 56–58.

CHAPTER 5

1. Frank Luntz and Donald Trump, "Trump asked if he had ever asked God for forgiveness," *The Family Leadership Summit* 2015 video, 2:08, July 18, 2015, https://www.c-span.org/video/?c4545095/trump-asked -ever-asked-god-forgiveness.

2. Paul Tillich, *The New Being* (New York: Scribner's, 1955), 9.

3. "Prayers of Confession, Assurance, and Pardon," *The United Methodist Hymnal*, #890.
4. Alexandr Solzhenitsyn, *The Gulag Archipelago* (New York: Harper and Row, 1976), part I, 168.
5. J. B. Phillips, *Your God Is Too Small: A Guide for Believers and Skeptics Alike* (New York: Touchstone, 2012), Kindle edition.
6. Paul Tillich, *The New Being*, 10.

CHAPTER 6
1. Paul Tillich, *The Shaking of the Foundations* (London: SCM Press, 1949), 170.
2. Thomas A. Dorsey, "Precious Lord, Take My Hand," *The United Methodist Hymnal*, #474. Hill & Range Songs, 1938; renewed Unichappell Music, Inc.
3. "The Apostles' Creed, Ecumenical Version," *The United Methodist Hymnal*, #882.

APPENDIX
1. John Norman Davidson Kelly, *Early Christian Creeds* (London: Longman, 1972), 102.
2. Philip Schaff, *The Creeds of Christendom*, vol. 2, *The Greek and Latin Creeds, with Translations* (New York: Harper & Brothers, 1877), 64.
3. "The Apostles' Creed, Ecumenical Version," *The United Methodist Hymnal*, #882.
4. Philip Schaff, *The Creeds of Christendom*, vol. 1, *The History of the Creeds*, 50.
5. "The Nicene Creed," *The United Methodist Hymnal* #880.
6. Schaff, *The Creeds of Christendom*, vol. 2, 89-94.
7. Schaff, *The Creeds of Christendom*, vol. 2, 96-99.

BIBLIOGRAPHY

The following are just a few of the nearly one hundred books on Christian theology that I've read over the years. I've chosen to list these because they are accessible and understandable to laypeople and pastors, whereas some of the texts on theology are less accessible.

These are the sorts of books I go back to from time to time to read. The list is not exhaustive, and I know there are many other outstanding volumes on Christian theology available, but I'm hoping this list will be a good starting point. The list reflects a faithfulness to Christian tradition and Scripture as well as a rigorous intellectual approach that I believe will be helpful to those with questions who are open to finding truth in Christianity. I have numerous volumes that are newer than these, but none that I return to as often.

Grenz, Stanley J. *Theology for the Community of God*. Grand
    Rapids: Eerdmans, 2000.
    Grenz died at the age of fifty-five in 2005, but his work
    continues to impact readers. He has sometimes been
    referred to as a "pioneer in postmodern evangelicalism"
    and was one of the most influential evangelical theologians
    of the late twentieth and early twenty-first centuries.

Guthrie, Shirley. *Christian Doctrine*. Louisville: Westminster/ John Knox, 1994.
Shirley Guthrie died in 2004, but his book on Christian doctrine continues to be a go-to resource for pastors and laity alike. Professor Guthrie was the J. B. Green Professor of Systematic Theology at Columbia Theological Seminary for forty years.

Lochman, Jan Milič. *The Faith We Confess: An Ecumenical Dogmatics*. Minneapolis: Augsburg Fortress, 1984.
This was a standard seminary text twenty-five years ago, but it does an excellent job of setting out an introduction to Christian theology. Lochman was professor of systematic theology at the University of Basel in Switzerland.

Macquarrie, John. *Principles of Christian Theology*. New York: Pearson, 1966 (2nd ed., 1977).
That this book is still in print fifty years after it was first published speaks to how many have found it helpful. Professor Macquarrie taught at Oxford; he died in 2007.

McGrath, Alister E. *Christian Theology: An Introduction*. Oxford: Blackwell, 2000.
McGrath is the Andreas Idreos Professor in Science and Religion at the University of Oxford.

Wright, N. T. *Simply Christian*. San Francisco: HarperSanFrancisco, 2006.
Wright is a retired Anglican bishop, New Testament scholar, professor of New Testament and Early Christianity at the University of St. Andrews, and popular author in the evangelical tradition.

ACKNOWLEDGMENTS

I'm grateful to Dr. Kendall Soulen, Professor of Systematic Theology at Candler Theological Seminary, Emory University; Dr. Roger Olsen, Professor of Theology at Truett Theological Seminary, Baylor University; and Dr. Timothy Bryan, Senior Adjunct Lecturer in Church History at Iliff School of Theology, for their review and suggestions of the first draft of this book. Their comments strengthened the book, and I'm most appreciative.

As always, I am grateful to Susan Salley and Ron Kidd for their partnership in making this book a reality. I'm also grateful for the outstanding team from United Methodist Communications and the members of Church of the Resurrection's staff and congregation who helped me to prepare the video that is available to accompany this book when it is used as a small group study. I'm grateful for the people of the Church of the Resurrection who have graciously allowed me to test the ideas in this book on them in my preaching, and who have allowed me time to write in the hope that this material will touch the lives of many.

Finally, as always, I want to express my deepest appreciation for my wife, LaVon Bandy Hamilton. She befriended me as a fourteen-year-old who didn't believe in God, and in the years since she has helped me to know God and to grow in my faith. She's been my constant companion on this faith journey, and I'm profoundly grateful for her partnership and love.

LEARN THE SIGNIFICANCE
AND THE POWER OF THE
PRAYER JESUS TAUGHT

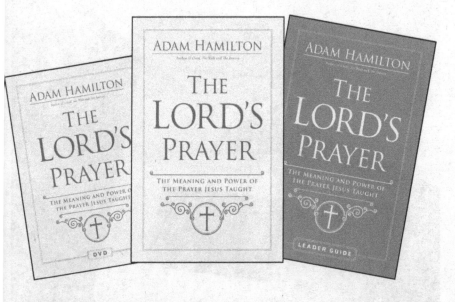

In *The Lord's Prayer: The Meaning and Power of the Prayer Jesus Taught* book and Bible study, best-selling author Adam Hamilton explores each of the prayer's rich lines and examines their meanings in the Bible, illuminating what we ask of God and what we ask of ourselves through its words. Not only will you come to understand its power; you'll learn how to use the Lord's Prayer as a pattern for all of your prayers.

EXPLORE THE STUDY AT
ADAMHAMILTON.COM/LORDSPRAYER.

Printed in the USA
CPSIA information can be obtained
at www.ICGtesting.com
LVHW030911050224
770748LV00006B/19